Practical Divinity
by William Fenner
with chapters by C. Matthew McMahon

Copyright Information

Practical Divinity, by William Fenner, with chapters by C. Matthew McMahon, Ph.D., Th.D.
Edited by Therese B. McMahon

© 2026 by Puritan Publications and A Puritan's Mind

Published by Puritan Publications
A Ministry of A Puritan's Mind in Crossville, TN
www.apuritansmind.com
www.puritanpublications.com
www.reformedsynod.com
www.gracechapeltn.com

All rights reserved. No part of this publication may be reproduced, stored in a retrieval system or transmitted in any form by any means, electronic, mechanical, photocopy, recording or otherwise, without the prior permission of the publisher, except as provided by USA copyright law.

First Electronic Edition, 2026
First Modern Print Edition, 2026
Manufactured in the United States of America

eISBN: 978-1-62663-540-1
ISBN: 978-1-62663-541-8

Table of Contents

William Fenner and the Glory of Practical Divinity . 4

Meet William Fenner 13

To the Reader.. 15

Outline of the Book 17

Sermon 1: The Misery of Earthly Thoughts 30

Sermon 2: A Sermon of Self-Denial 49

Sermon 3: The Efficacy of Importunate Prayer Part 1 71

Sermon 4: The Efficacy of Importunate Prayer Part 2 88

Sermon 5: The Necessity of Gospel-Obedience Part 1 106

Sermon 6: The Necessity of Gospel Obedience Part 2 125

Sermon 7: A Caveat Against Late Repentance 138

Sermon 8: The Sovereign Virtue of the Gospel........ 159

Sermon 9: A Funeral Sermon 186

Sermon 10: The Signs of God's Forsaking a People 203

Other Works Published by Puritan Publications . 228

William Fenner and the Glory of Practical Divinity
by C. Matthew McMahon, Ph.D., Th.D.

There are books that sparkle, but do not warm; sermons that stir the mind, but sometimes do not bind the conscience; treatises that argue, but do not *shepherd*. And then, sometimes, one stumbles into the work of a preacher who lived in the very marrow of Christ's gospel, and who pressed it with such holy bluntness that his sermons strike like hammer blows, and at the same time, drip like honey from the Rock. William Fenner was such a man. His *Practical Divinity* is not a dusty relic of the seventeenth century, but a burning coal laid on the lips of the Church. He is a divine who makes doctrine bleed into conduct, who makes theology pray, who makes the word of God live in the very sinews of ordinary Christians.

Fenner was no speculative schoolman. He was a preacher with his feet planted in the mud of Essex, but his head full of Scripture, and his heart chained to the throne of Christ. His sermons are "practical" in the noblest sense of the word. He never lets truth float like a wandering cloud. He *nails* it down. He *drives* it into the conscience; like a dying man to dying men. He will have none of the shallow Christianity that nods politely to the Almighty on Sunday and then puts Him out of mind for the rest of the week. He preaches so that men tremble, repent, and actually live for God.

Brokenness and the Medicine of Grace

One of the strongest sections of his preaching is on the broken heart. He lays out with all the vigor of a prophet that God will not heal until He has *broken*. "Comfortable cordials before the time have been the damnation of many souls," Fenner warns, and he is right. He is *not* content with sentimental religion. He insists that the corrosive of conviction must eat deep before the balm of Christ is applied (Psalm 34:18; Isaiah 57:15). This is not cruelty; it is the physician's wisdom. Give a sweet draught before the poison is purged, and you kill the patient. Fenner had seen too many men pluck out the arrows of conviction too soon, only to have their wounds fester for years, sometimes *decades*.

Here is no pampering preacher who tells sinners to pat themselves on the back because they feel a little sorrow. No, Fenner is after the *marrow* of the soul. He will not mistake half-humiliation for true repentance. What good is *a cake half turned*? He says many men are "half in their sins, and half out, like a stick half in the water and half out, which seems broken but is not." His point is sharp as glass: brokenness that does not break with sin is no brokenness at all. Zacchaeus is his exhibit (Luke 19:8). When grace seized that little tax collector, his sins flew off, not with dripping reluctance but gushing restitution. *Half* measures had no place. And Fenner presses his hearers, *Do you see sins dropping away in flakes, or do you only play at sorrow while clutching your idols?*

This is *practical* divinity. People want divinity. They want religion to an extent. Do they want *practical* religion? It is the anatomy of repentance, the surgery of the Spirit described in detail so that no one mistakes a scratch for a mortal wound, or a half-turn for conversion. In a day where men are quick to patch, Fenner slows us down. Let the corrosive work. Better to bleed a while under God's hand than to leap into false peace and rot.

Wildness, Pride, and the Saddle of God

Fenner is also brilliant in his use of earthy images. He will not let us drift in abstractions. He tells us the heart must be broken not only from sin's guilt but from its wildness. "Man is born like a wild ass's colt" (Job 11:12). If God has not tamed you, you are still wild. He brings in Calvin's comparison: you are not fit for God's saddle if you buck off every exhortation and bolt at every reproof. What a picture! Fenner makes the proud man see himself as a mule resisting the bridle, and the humbled man as one who finally bows under the rein of the Almighty (Psalm 32:9).

This theme of *taming* runs straight into his treatment of pride. He calls pride the neck that must be broken, the very root of sin. "The word has not broken the heart until it has broken the neck of this pride of thine," he says. That is plain preaching. He flays the self-serving excuses of those who plead necessity for lying, drunkenness, Sabbath-breaking, and then dares them to call that anything but execrable pride (Jeremiah 13:15; Psalm 10:4). He ridicules the man who bows and kneels in prayer but refuses to stoop to God's commandments. This is a scalpel: sin is not a trifle, it is rebellion rooted in arrogant self-love.

Fenner will not let you off until you see that pride is not just a spot of vanity in your dress, but a direct defiance of the living God. He shows that until you count it your glory to be reproached for Christ, you are still swollen with self. Here again the *practical divinity*: he turns doctrine of depravity into a whip that strikes our backs until we cry for grace.

Death, Judgment, and the Weight of Eternity

Fenner's funeral sermons are as serious as the grave. Preaching on Isaiah 57:1, "The righteous perisheth, and no man layeth it to heart"—he reminds his hearers that death is no respecter of persons. The righteous die as surely as the wicked. He stacks the texts high: "Your fathers, where are they? and the prophets, do they live for ever?" (Zechariah 1:5). "How dieth the wise man? as the fool," (Ecclesiastes 2:16). "It is appointed unto men once to die, but after this the judgment," (Hebrews 9:27). And he rubs it in: you must die, even you who are godly, even you who pray and preach.

But he does not leave it there. He explains with *precision (oh those precisionists!)* that Christ has *abolished* the sting of death (1 Corinthians 15:55–57). Death remains, but its tyranny is gone. It no longer executes the curse, it ferries the saint into glory. Fenner is careful, he knows men will twist the doctrine into carnal security. So he insists the righteous die, but not in the same way. For them death is a *passage*, not a prison. And then he turns it to application: if the righteous perish, we ought to lay it to heart, mourn their absence, and tremble at what judgments their removal might signify. This is classic Christian pastoral theology. Death is never handled abstractly. It is pressed into holy uses. It is meant to wean us from love of this present world (Genesis 3:19; Romans 6:23), to prepare us for the better country, and to grieve us when the righteous are removed because their absence exposes us to God's judgments (Isaiah 57:1–2; Jeremiah 5:1). Fenner takes what every funeral forces upon the mind and then makes it impossible to shrug off.

God Departing from a People

Perhaps the most terrifying portion of Fenner's work is his sermon on Jeremiah 14:9: "And we are called by thy name; leave us not." Here his voice is like thunder rolling over a country's fields. He insists that God may unchurch a nation, may withdraw his ordinances, may leave a people to darkness. He points to Shiloh, once the

Introduction – The Glory of Practical Divinity

place of God's name, now a ruin (Jeremiah 7:12–14). He points to Pergamos and Thyatira, once shining lampstands, now smoldering ashes (Revelation 1:11). He warns that God can sue out a bill of divorce against a people (Hosea 1:9; 2:2).

And then he applies it home. Why not our own country? Have we not the same sins as Jerusalem? Are we better than Sodom? Do we not abuse God's patience? Have we not turned his mercies into wantonness? Fenner cries, God is packing up his gospel because none will buy his wares. He sees the Puritan exodus to New England as God shipping away his Noahs and Lots, leaving his home country of England ripe for judgment.

This is the *Reformed* vision of covenant applied. Outward covenant membership does not secure a nation if there is no repentance. Ordinances can be withdrawn. Candlesticks can be removed. God may be a husband no longer if we persist in whoredoms. Fenner makes it plain: if God goes, our glory goes. "The glory is departed from Israel," (1 Samuel 4:22). And England must know the same can be true of her, as with any country.

Keeping God Present

Yet even in this thunder, Fenner shows the way back. He tells his hearers that to keep the Lord, they must prepare him a room (2 Corinthians 6:17), give him service by pure worship (Isaiah 5:4–5), welcome him heartily, and plead importunately that he stay (Genesis

32:24–26). He paints the picture of Moses, who would not go to Canaan without God's presence (Exodus 33:14–15), and David, who panted for God's ordinances (Psalm 42:1). He mocks those who say once a week is too much, who grow weary of ordinances. He says they are weary of God Himself. He warns that such men will one day get their desire: God will depart, and they shall be thrust down to hell (Job 22:17; Matthew 11:23).

This is no tame sermonizing. It is an importunate plea: cling to God, clasp Him like Mary clung to Christ, do not let Him go. It is practical divinity because it does not stop at doctrine—it turns every truth into a summons to holy desperation. Fenner will not allow the gospel to be "kept with lazy wishes." He insists on knees to the floor, hearts to the throne, households reformed, sins cut off, ordinances prized, and Christ retained.

Why Fenner Matters

What makes Fenner's *Practical Divinity* so "awesome," to use a modern word that he himself would likely spit out, is precisely this: it marries theology and life. It is doctrine driven into conduct with biblical nails of iron. It is *Puritan experimental theology* at its sharpest, testing men, dividing marrow from bone, showing who is truly broken and who is merely play-acting.

His *Caveat Against Late Repentance*, may be one of the best sermons I've ever heard, and it's certainly one of the best I've heard in the last few years. This kind of

Introduction – The Glory of Practical Divinity

preaching is what is lost in our day. He is unsparing toward hypocrisy, but tender toward the wounded. He is bold in warning nations, but earnest in wooing souls. He takes the whole sweep of Scripture—Job, Psalms, Prophets, Gospels, Epistles—and uses it not as a scholar's adornment, but as a shepherd's crook. He drags the sheep away from cliffs, and he clubs the wolves who would devour them.

Today, often, so very often, men *toy* with gospel truths. Fenner teaches us what "practical divinity" means. It is not light advice for self-improvement. It is the living application of God's eternal truth to the conscience, so that sinners are broken, saints are built, and Christ is magnified. It is theology that bleeds, groans, warns, comforts, and prays. It is divinity that walks into the sickroom, stands at the graveside, storms the throne of grace, and will not let go of God.

Read Fenner, and you hear a man who believed God was present in preaching. You hear a man who knew death was at the door, sin was in the heart, and Christ was the only balm. You hear the Puritan genius: Scripture quoted, doctrine unfolded, conscience pressed, Christ exalted. It is a shame that so many Christians today think "practical divinity" means three tips for a happy marriage or five keys to stress reduction. Fenner would laugh bitterly at such *drivel*. For him, practical divinity meant living and dying in the presence of God, tamed from wildness, broken from pride, parted from sin, trembling at death, longing for Christ, clinging to ordinances, and pleading that God not depart.

William Fenner was no fool preacher. He was a faithful ambassador of the King, a man whose sermons still throb with fire. His *Practical Divinity* is indeed a treasure, not because it is quaint or old, but because it is true, scriptural, and relentlessly aimed at the conscience. The Church today, fattened on amusements and softened by ease, needs nothing more than to sit again under such thunder. Where is that thunder? Let Fenner's voice ring once more, for it is the very voice of practical, Reformed, biblical Christianity.

In Christ's grace and mercy,
C. Matthew McMahon, Ph.D., Th.D.
From My study, September, 2025
"...search the Scriptures..." (John 5:39).
www.apuritansmind.com
www.puritanpublications.com
www.gracechapeltn.com
www.reformedsynod.com

Meet William Fenner
By C. Matthew McMahon, Ph.D., Th.D.

William Fenner (1600–1640) was an eminent Puritan divine, born in 1600. He received his education at Pembroke Hall, Cambridge, and later took his degree in divinity at Oxford. He first entered upon his settled ministry at Sedgley in Staffordshire, where the Lord greatly blessed his labors. The church, being both large and populous, had been in a state of deep ignorance and ungodliness; but through Fenner's holy life and faithful preaching over a period of *four* years, many were turned to righteousness. When he was at length forced to leave—most likely because of his nonconformity—and was replaced by a weak vicar, *ignorance and sin* soon returned to the parish.

Fenner had a natural and earnest care for souls. Beyond the faithful attention he gave to his own flock, he delighted in preaching the gospel in many places. He was often sought out as a casuist, giving counsel on cases of conscience, and was highly esteemed by persons of rank, particularly the Earl of Warwick, who became his great friend and patron. In 1629 the Earl presented him to the rectory of Rochford in Essex, where he remained until his death. His life and labors brought much honor to the grace of God.

Fenner did not waste his ministry on dry disputes about outward rites and ceremonies, but instead fed his hearers with *the sincere milk of the word*. Historians record that "he was much admired and followed by the puritanical party."

He died around 1640 at the age of *forty*. Edmund Calamy, later one of the ejected ministers of 1662, succeeded him at Rochford.

Fenner's writings display a deep acquaintance with true religion in all its parts, and his manner of preaching and writing was plain, fervent, and searching.

Main Works of William Fenner, including minor works:
1. The Riches of Grace (1641)
2. A Treatise of Affections (1642)
3. Christ's Alarm to Drowsy Sinners (1650)
4. Practical Divinity (1660)
5. A Divine Message to the Elect Soul (1651)
6. Of Willful Impenitency (1651)
7. Of Conscience (1651)
8. Hidden Manna (1652)

Mett William Fenner

To the Reader

Christian Reader,

The author of the sermons now in your hand was well known to many (and in part to myself) as a man fully fitted and tempered to be a minister of the gospel, being furnished with two sovereign ingredients: *light and heat*. He had both eminent knowledge in the things of God, and also, great strength and fervency of zeal to manage that knowledge to the best advantage for the glory of God. That crown of honor which our Savior Himself set upon the head of John the Baptist would very well—without the least flattery—have fitted his also: "He was a burning and a shining light," (John 5:35). And although his sense and mine do not agree in every particular touched on in the sermons following, yet I judge the reading of them to be a worthy recompense for any person's time and labor that shall be spent upon them.

The God of peace grant us, in His time, union of judgment in the truth, and in the meantime union of affections in that which is good. If we truly and heartily love peace, and not merely our own thoughts and wills under a mistaken notion of peace, it is most certain that we will not suffer it to be taken from us by any difference in judgment whatsoever.

I would only keep your heart and spirit from better company in the sermons that follow by means of this short epistle. That which hinders you in this matter will immediately be removed after the speaking of this one word: Read, understand, and consider, and your soul shall prosper, and the grace of God in Christ shall be your portion.

Yours in the service of truth and peace,
JOHN GOODWIN
Coleman Street, London.
February 5, 1646.

Outline of the Book

Text: Isaiah 55:7

[Doctrine.] Those whose minds or thoughts run habitually on earthly things are yet in the state of misery.

[Reason 1] Because a man is in the state of misery until he has repented, and until a man has forsaken his vain thoughts, he has not repented.

[Reason 2] Because a man is in a state of misery until he is in Christ, and a man is not in Christ until his thoughts are sanctified.

[Reason 3] Because a man is in the state of misery that does not love God, and a man can never love God until he forsakes his vain thoughts.

[Reason 4] Because that man is in a state of misery that does not forsake sin, and a man can never forsake sin until he leaves his vain thoughts.

1. Because vain thoughts are great sins.
2. They are sins of the highest part of man.
3. They are the breach of every commandment.
4. Because they are the strength of a man's soul, the firstborn of original corruption.
5. Because they are the dearest acts of man.

[Doctrine. 2] It is hard for men to forsake their sinful thoughts.

1. Because it is hard to reform the inward part.
2. Because thoughts are partial acts and run on in every action.

3. Because thoughts are inward, in the heart.

[Use 1] For men to examine their thoughts.

A man may know whether he is a child of God, or of the Devil, by his thoughts.

1. Because men's thoughts are the free acts of their hearts.
2. They are the immediate acts of the heart.
3. They are continued acts of the heart.
4. They are the univocal acts of the heart.
5. They are the swiftest acts of the heart.
6. They are the peculiar acts of the heart.
7. They are the greatest accusers or excusers of the heart.

[Use 2] For direction. If sin in thought is so great, how horrible then is sin in the act?

[Use 3] For exhortation to consider:

1. What great reason we have to set our thoughts on God.
2. What thoughts they are that God calls for.

Text: Luke 9:23

[Doctrine.] The words of the text unfolded and opened in several particulars.

The first action to be performed of every Christian is to deny himself.

[Reason 1] From Christ's example, He denied Himself.

[Reason 2] Christ denied Himself for us; therefore, we must deny ourselves for Him.

[Reason 3] This Christ enjoins to all that will come after Him.

What is meant by a man's self:
1. A man's corrupt will, wit, and reason.
2. All his lusts and corruptions.
3. Not only a man's corrupt self, but even a man's good self in some respects.

Self-denying is opposite to self-seeking.

There are five things in self-seeking:
1. It is a head-lust.
    1. Because it is a leading lust to all lust.
    2. Because self is the cause of all other lusts of the heart.
    3. Because self is an in-lust; it runs along through all the lusts of the flesh.
    4. Self is a make-lust; a man would never break out into lust were it not for self.
    5. Self is a lust that is in request.
2. Self-seeking is a self-conceited lust.
    1. When a man has a conceit of himself.
    2. Of his own gifts.
    3. Of his own actions.
    4. Of the state that he is in.

When as a self-conceited man:
1. Has no real worth in himself.
2. Will not stand to the judgment of those that can judge him.
3. Has too high a conceit of himself.
4. Rests in the judgment of himself.

The reasons of this are:
1. Because sinners are fools.
2. Men are born fools.
3. Men are well conceited of their own estate.
4. The Lord gives up many to a spirit of slumber.

The woeful case of a self-conceited man:
1. Because the Scripture calls self-conceit—
    1. Only a thinking.
    2. A superstition.
    3. A shadow.
    4. An imagination.
    5. An appearance.
2. So long as a man is well conceited of himself, Christ has no commission to call him.
3. Christ rejoices that He has no commission to call such.
4. The self-conceited man is in the broad way to hell.

Text: Luke 11:9
The opening of the context.
The words of the text opened.
[Doctrine.] Importunate prayer is a restless prayer.
[Reason 1] It will take no primitive denial; it must have some answer.
[Reason 2] Not a positive denial, not a contrary answer.
[Reason 3] It will take no reproachful repulse.
[Reason 4] It is, in a holy manner, a kind of impudent prayer.

Reasons why we must seek importunately:
1. In regard of God's majesty—God respects it.
2. In regard of God's mercy—it is a disgrace to God's mercy to beg it coldly.
3. In regard of ourselves—else we would never esteem mercy.

Reasons why men are not importunate in prayer:
1. Because men account prayer a penance.
2. Most men content themselves with formality.
3. Men are gentleman beggars.
4. Men have wrong conceits of prayer:
    1. They have high conceits of their own prayers.
    2. They have low conceits of their sins.
    3. They have base thoughts of God.
    4. They have wrong conceits of importunity.

Signs whereby we may know whether our prayers are importunate:
1. Importunate prayer is always the prayer of an importunate man.
2. It is the prayer of a pure conscience.
3. It is a prayer that is full of strong arguments.
4. It is a striving prayer.
5. It is a wakeful prayer.
6. It is an assurance-getting prayer.

Marks of prayer that is not importunate:
1. It is a lazy prayer.
2. It is not poured out from the heart.

3. It is a praying only by fits.
4. It is a silent prayer, omitting that which should most be insisted upon.
5. It is a seldom prayer.
6. It is a lukewarm prayer.
7. By-thoughts in prayer keep prayer from being importunate.

By-thoughts in prayer arise:
1. From corrupt nature.
2. From nature as it is encumbered.
3. From Satan.
4. From spiritual sluggishness.

Motives to importunate prayer:
1. Because prayer enables a man for duties.
2. Prayer is the compendium of all divinity.
3. Prayer is a man's utmost reference.
4. Prayer is that which God's people have, though they have nothing else.
5. Prayer has the command of mercy.
6. Prayer is God's delight.
7. Importunate prayer is a willing prayer.
8. Importunate prayer is the only faithful prayer.

Helps to importunity in prayer:
1. Labor to know your own misery.
2. Be sensible of your misery.
3. Observe how God's people pray.
4. Get a store of prayer.
5. Labor to be full of good works.
6. Labor to reform your household.

Text: Colossians 1:10
[Doctrine.] Those that profess Christ must walk worthy of Christ.
[Reason 1] Because it is Christ that calls us to be Christians.
[Reason 2] Because it is the gospel of Christ whereby we are called.
[Reason 3] Because by the gospel we are called to repentance.
[Reason 4] Because if we do not walk worthy of Christ, God will not hold us to be His servants.
[Reason 5] If we do not walk worthy of Christ, then it will be for the glory of God to cashier us.
[Reason 6] If we do not walk worthy of Christ, we put indignity upon Him.
Motives to walk worthy of God:
1. If we do walk worthy of God, then we shall answer all the labor and cost that God has expended on us.
2. Then we shall walk with God in white.
3. Then we do not disappoint God's account.
4. Then we shall be importunate beggars, and so worthy of mercy.
5. Then we shall add humiliation to every duty we perform.

If we do not walk worthy of God, then:
1. We walk worthy of destruction.
2. We are guilty of the death of Christ.

3. We shall be condemned.

The second part of the text opened:

[Doctrine.] It is possible to walk in all manner of pleasing unto the Lord.

[Reason 1] Because God is a righteous God.

[Reason 2] There is a way, wherein if we walk, we shall please God.

[Reason 3] The Lord has shown us this way.

[Doctrine. 4] Many have walked in this way before us. It is a fit duty to please God:

[Reason 1] Because God is a great God.

[Reason 2] His pleasure is a good pleasure.

[Reason 3] Christ, who is our better, did those things that pleased God.

[Reason 4] If we do not please God, our consciences will condemn us.

[Reason 5] It is a duty most suitable to human society.

[Doctrine.] Pleasing of God is a large duty.

[Reason 1] It is the end of all our duties.

[Reason 2] It is the most acceptable of all duties.

[Reason 3] It is unconfinable to place or time.

[Reason 4] It is in all things without limitation.

[Reason 5] It is an everlasting duty.

[Reason 6] It is the whole duty of the new man.

[Doctrine.] It is a necessary duty to please God.

[Reason 1] Because we have no saving grace unless we labor to please God.

[Reason 2] We are in a woeful case if we do not please God.

[Reason 3] If we do not please God, we are continually in danger of His wrath.

[Use] To condemn:
1. Those that please not God.
2. Those that please men.
3. Those that please themselves.

Text: Luke 23:24

[Doctrine.] Extraordinary cases never make a common rule.

That a wicked life will have a cursed end—this is the ordinary rule. Yet in some extraordinary cases it may be otherwise:
1. When God is pleased to show His prerogative royal.
2. When a sinner has not had means of salvation in his life, but only at his death.
3. When a sinner shall be made exemplary.
4. When the Lord may be as much honored by a man's death as He has been dishonored by his life.

This repentance of the thief was extraordinary:
1. Because it was one of the wonders of Christ's passion.
2. Because we read not of any other that was converted at the last as the thief was.
3. Because of the suddenness of it.
4. In regard of the evangelical perfection of it, containing:

1. His penitential confession.
2. His penitential profession.
3. His penitential satisfaction.
4. His penitential self-denial.
5. His penitential faith.
6. His penitential resolution.
7. His penitential prayer.

5. This repentance was extraordinary in regard of the incomparableness of it.

[Use] To condemn those that rely upon this example. This example is once recorded that none might despair, and but once that none might presume.

None should defer their repentance because of this thief's example:

1. Because this thief had not the means of life and grace before.
2. Because we never read that this thief put off his repentance until the last.
3. Because at that time God was in a way of working miracles.

Text: Psalm 147:3
The words of the text opened.
What is meant by wholeness of heart.
What is meant by brokenness of heart.
[Doctrine.] Christ justifies and sanctifies, or heals, the brokenhearted.
[Reason 1] Because God has given grace unto Christ to heal the brokenhearted.

[Reason 2] Christ has undertaken to do it.
[Reason 3] Christ has this in charge to bind up the brokenhearted.
[Reason 4] None but the brokenhearted will accept of Christ.
Several objections are answered.
Reasons why Christ will heal the brokenhearted:
1. This is the most seasonable time to be healed—when the heart is broken.
2. It is the most profitable time.
3. It is the very critical time; the heart can never be healed until it is broken.

Signs of a broken heart:
1. A breaking from sin.
2. A breaking in itself with sorrow.
3. When the heart is broken, then it will stoop to God's word in all things.

The history of Zacchaeus's conversion is opened in several particulars.

Text: Isaiah 57:1
[Doctrine.] All men must die.
[Reason 1] Because God has appointed it.
[Reason 2] Because all men and women are of the dust.
[Reason 3] Because all have sinned.
[Reason 4] Because as death came into the world by sin, so sin might go out of the world by death.
Objections against this are answered.

[Use 1] Let no man look to be exempted from death for his righteousness.

[Use 2] We should learn to draw our hearts from this present world.

[Use 3] To teach us to prepare ourselves for a better life.

The death and loss of good men must be laid to heart as an especial cause of grief and sorrow:

[Reason 1] Because the instruments of God's glory are taken away.

[Reason 2] Because of the great loss that others have by their death.

[Reason 3] Because of the evil to come; for while they live, they are as a wall to keep off the wrath of God.

[Use 1] To reprove those who rejoice at the death of the righteous.

[Doctrine. 2] To inform us what a loss it is when the righteous are taken away.

When God will bring any great judgment upon a people or nation, He ordinarily takes away His faithful servants from among them.

[Use 1] To inform us of God's extraordinary love to His children.

[Use 2] To inform us that when the righteous are taken away, we are certainly to expect some great judgment from God to fall upon us.

Text: Jeremiah 14:9
The opening of the context in many particulars.

[Doctrine.] God many times does cast off a people.
Signs of God's casting off a people:
1. When He takes away His love and respect from a people.
2. When He takes away His providence from them.
3. When He breaks down the walls of magistracy and ministry.
4. When He takes away the benefit of both these helps.

[Use 1] To teach us to cast off security.

[Doctrine.] It is the importunate desire of the saints of God still to keep God present with them.

The presence of God is the particular favor of God which He expresses in His ordinances.

Questions answered:
1. Whether a man may be saved without preaching.
2. Who they are that are weary of God.

To rebuke God's people for their neglect in not striving to keep God, who seems to be departing.

How may we keep the Lord among us?
1. We must be sure to prepare a room for Him.
2. We must give Him content.
3. We must make Him welcome.
4. We must be importunate with God to stay, and account it a great favor if He will remain.

Sermon 1:
The Misery of Earthly Thoughts

Isaiah 55:7, "Let the wicked forsake his way, and the unrighteous man his thoughts: and let him return unto the LORD, and he will have mercy upon him; and to our God, for he will abundantly pardon."

I have previously begun the doctrine of the thoughts of men in another series. Now I desire to finish it. From this text we gathered this point:

[Doctrine.] Those whose minds run habitually on earthly things are yet in the state of misery.

First, because a man is in the state of misery until he has repented. Now until a man has forsaken his old thoughts, that man has not repented. "O Jerusalem, wash thine heart from wickedness, that thou mayest be saved. How long shall thy vain thoughts lodge within thee?" (Jeremiah 4:14). A man must not only rid himself of vain thoughts, but he must wash his heart clean with this emphasis—that he may be saved. There is no salvation without this.

Second, as a man is in the state of misery until he has repented, so also until he is in Christ. Now when a man is led by his own vain thoughts, his thoughts being not sanctified, that man is not in Christ. If he were in Christ, Christ would sanctify his thoughts. "Yes, but he has wronged me," says someone, "therefore I will think thus and thus." No, but Christ casts down the strongholds, and if you will not yield, Christ will cast you off. But if you belong to Christ, He will cast all down before you.

Third, that man is in the state of misery who does not love God, who does not walk with God in his thoughts. "Jesus said unto him, Thou shalt love the Lord thy God with all thy heart, and with all thy soul, and with all thy mind," (Matthew 22:37). "So I do," says one, "and yet I think on my vanities too." In this way carnal men *think* they love God. But if you love God with all your heart, you love Him with all *that is in* your heart. For what is a man's heart, but the purposes of his heart? Now if a man does not give up vain purposes, he does not love God with all his heart.

Fourth, that man that cannot forsake sin is in the state of misery and can never enter into life. As the text says, "Let the wicked forsake his way." A man must deny his own words and speak according to God's warrant. The actions of men's lives are the ways of their thoughts. The tongue must not only forsake its way, but the heart also; otherwise a man is wicked. "The thoughts of the wicked are an abomination to the LORD: but the words of the pure are pleasant words," (Proverbs 15:26). He is wicked whose thoughts are not sanctified. But what will men say? Shall we be condemned for a thought? Words are small sins, and thoughts are less. Must a man then so strictly look to his thoughts? I will make it plain that for a man to be given to vain thoughts is a grievous sin.

1. Because if the sin of vain thoughts is pardoned, it will ask abundance of mercy. Mark the text: "for he will abundantly pardon," (Isaiah 55:7). No repentance, no mercy, *without* abundance. Therefore, it is not as small as the world takes it to be.
2. Thoughts are the sins of the highest part of a man, for they are the sins of the heart; and surely the sins of the chiefest part are greater than any other. A king does not count it much for a rogue to steal by the roadside, but for a knight or nobleman it is a foul matter. So, the Lord would not have the lordly part to sin against Him. He would not have the tongue sin, much less the heart, which is the kingly part of a man. This is the reason why Deborah calls them "great thoughts of heart," (Judges 5:15). Sins in thought are great sins. The heart is the lady, the mistress, the highest part of a man; and He that made us looks that we should serve Him with the master part, and that must be given to Him.
3. Because thoughts are breaches of every commandment. Other sins are but against one, but all the commandments condemn vain thoughts. The first commandment says, "Thou shalt have no other gods before me," (Exodus 20:3). But you set an image up in your heart when you think on your pleasures, *etc*. Again, "Remember the sabbath day, to keep it holy,"

(Exodus 20:8). Now if you think your own thoughts on that day, you break this commandment. And so it is with all the rest. *The sin of thought is therefore a heinous sin.*

4. Because they are the strength of a man's heart and soul, the firstborn of original corruption. A man by nature is a child of wrath, a soul and a body of death. Now what does the heart first break out in? It first shows itself in its thoughts. And if it is the firstborn, it must needs be the strength, as Jacob said to Reuben his firstborn, he was his strength (Genesis 49:3). Therefore, all lordship lies in the heart. A man may more easily part with all other sins than with this, because the bent of the heart runs this way. The heart will part with any sin rather than with its pernicious thoughts.

5. Because they are the *dearest* acts of men. We count a man preferred when he is preferred to the thoughts of another. "But think on me when it shall be well with thee," (Genesis 40:14), said Joseph to Pharaoh's butler. I count it thanks enough if you prefer me to your thoughts. We prize that most which we *think* most on. That which a man scorns, he scorns to bestow his thoughts on; but that which a man sets his heart on, that is his darling. Now that anything should be dear to a man besides God is a horrible sin—when a man makes his dog his darling, his harlot

his darling, etc. For look at what you think most on: that is your darling, because you dandle it in your heart. Therefore, it is a horrible sin for a man not to set his heart upon God.

[Objection.] But can a man live without thoughts? Does grace call us to leave thinking? Then a man must cease to be.

[Answer.] *Non tollit, sed attollit naturam* (it does not take away, but it lifts up nature). God does not say, "Let the wicked forsake thoughts," but "his thoughts." Let him set them on other matters. When God calls men to Him, He is so far from taking away men's thoughts, that He will rather increase them. If you are a new creature, you must have more thoughts. You are full of thoughts now, but then you will be fuller. "I thought on my ways, and turned my feet unto thy testimonies," (Psalm 119:59). When David turned to God, his heart thought upon his ways. The word in the original implies *he thought on his ways on both sides*. The curious work of the sanctuary was wrought on both sides; common works are wrought only on one side, but on the other side are full of ends and shreds. So the prophet looks on his way on both sides; he strives to walk carefully, precisely, and accurately to turn himself to God's testimonies.

Therefore, God does not call us to forsake thoughts but to forsake our thoughts.

It is a hard duty for men to forsake their own thoughts. I will make it *appear so*:

Sermon 1: The Misery of Earthly Thoughts

First, because it is a hard thing to reform *oneself*. One thing may reform another, but here is the difficulty—for a thing to reform itself. It is an easy matter for a man's heart to reform his tongue, but it is hard for the heart to reform itself, in correcting its own thoughts. It is hard for a man to deny himself. A hell-hound may reform his tongue, but here is the difficulty, for his heart to reform itself. For thoughts are the heart. "Whose end is destruction, whose God is their belly, and whose glory is in their shame, who mind earthly things," (Philippians 3:19). Thoughts of earthly things are called the mind; a man's thoughts and his mind are all one. So that if the heart reforms thoughts, it must reform itself. Second, it is hard to reform thoughts because they are partial acts. If they were full acts, a man might reform them more easily. My reason is because they are in every action he does; thoughts run on in all men's actions. If thoughts stood alone, men might mend them; but they busy themselves about all actions. If a man prays, thoughts run along with him in prayer. No, men pray with twisted thoughts, so that before he comes to the end of his prayer, he will have abundance of glances on other things. See it in old Eli: "And it came to pass, as she continued praying before the LORD, that Eli marked her mouth. Now Hannah, she spake in her heart; only her lips moved, but her voice was not heard: therefore Eli thought she had been drunken," (1 Samuel 1:12-13). Either he was, or should have been, praying also; yet you see he had wandering thoughts to mark the lips of his neighbor. So when John was preaching, "And think not to say within yourselves, We have Abraham to our father: for I say unto you, that God is able of these stones to raise up children unto Abraham," (Matthew 3:9). There came a thought into his hearers' hearts that they were the seed of Abraham. What made them *think* so? John spoke of no such matter, but said, "Every tree which bringeth not forth good fruit is hewn down, and cast into the fire," (Matthew 3:10). They had, it seems, by-thoughts in the duty of hearing. Therefore, since thoughts in this way twist themselves about men's actions, it is hard to root them out.

Third, it is hard for men to forsake their own thoughts because they are in men's hearts. "Their inward thought is, that their houses shall continue for ever, and their dwelling places to all generations; they call their lands after their own names," (Psalm 49:11). Every man has two kinds of thoughts: inward and outward; explicit and implicit. Implicit thoughts are those that never show themselves in the heart except at some desperate attempt. Explicit are those which are in the heart every day. As in Psalm 49:11, men think their houses will continue forever. Would you think that men should have such thoughts, when their outward thoughts were that they were mortal? We see, says the text, that men die; and yet inwardly they think they will live forever. Now according to these inward thoughts men act, and therefore it is that men neglect repentance and other holy duties, as if God would never call them to account.

They do not have these thoughts rightly thought, but they are inward, and these spoil the heart. These are the causes why men cannot forsake their own thoughts.

Epiphanius speaks of a fig tree which grew in a wall. So bad thoughts will always be seizing on a man until he dies, and then "his breath goeth forth, he returneth to his earth; in that very day his thoughts perish," (Psalm 146:4). But so long as a man is alive in old Adam, these thoughts are rooted in the bottom of the soul, which hinder good duties; and this is the cause why vanity of mind sprouts up.

[Use.] Examine yourselves then; for it is one of the best ways for a man to try his estate, even to examine his thoughts. If a man would see whether the sea is salt, he need not drink all the water that is in it; one drop will serve his turn. So a man may see whether he is a child of God or of the Devil, even by his thoughts. I will make it appear by these reasons:

First, because men's thoughts are the free acts of their hearts. Many times you do not speak as you would, you do not act as you would, but a man thinks always as he will. The favor of great men, and the desire to please them, makes men do many things which they would not; but thoughts are free. I may say this or that, but I will think what I please. Therefore, if you will judge a man, judge him by what he does freely, and not by what he does by compulsion. But your thoughts are free, they are your own act; nothing can force your thoughts but yourself. Therefore, in them your heart shows itself, whether it is carnal or spiritual.

When Peter denied his Master, could a man have judged him by that, then he might have judged him an apostate. But that was his passion; he revealed what his *fear* was, *not what his heart was*. For if a man might have but looked into Peter's heart (though it was a fearful sin, and without God's mercy might have damned him), yet there you might have heard him say, "Oh, it is my Master! Oh, that I had never come here! It is my Master and Savior, I have none but Him." It was for fear of his life that he denied Him. "For as he thinketh in his heart, so is he," (Proverbs 23:7). A covetous usurer may make a rich feast, and say with his tongue, "Sir, you are welcome." He must give good words—the shame of the world and the speech of people will make him do it. Yet his thoughts may not be toward you. Search yourself, how do your thoughts go? Where do they go at home or abroad? Are your thoughts on heaven and heavenly things, or are they below? Surely, if a man's thoughts were on heavenly things, then his heart would be there also; for as a man thinks, so is he (Proverbs 23:7).

Second, as they are the freest acts, so they are the immediate acts of the heart. Can a man judge of the fountain by the water that runs seven miles off, as well as by that which runs immediately from it? The water seven miles off may have tincture from the soil, and so it may be bad there, though good at the fountain's head. Therefore, judge of the fountain by the water which comes immediately from it. Now thoughts come immediately from the heart. "For from within, out of the heart of men, proceed evil thoughts..." (Mark 7:21). Other sins come from the heart too, but at the second, third, or fourth hand; abundance of circumstances come between them and the act. As in the act of murder, there may have been base words offered, yes, and blows too, *etc*. But thoughts come immediately from the heart. Therefore, if your thoughts are proud, carnal, etc., so are you. If your thoughts carry you away in the cares of this life, so is your heart.

Third, thoughts are the continued acts of the heart; a man is always engaged in them. Can a man judge of a usurer, and say he is liberal, because he makes one great feast for his neighbors? No; but he may say it is a usurer's feast, a great feast. Judge a man by what he always does. You are not always praying, or in good company; but you are always thinking good or evil thoughts. Your thoughts are the continued acts of your heart. Can a man judge a horse for stumbling once in a long journey? At such a place he went well, and at such a time, and always; yet perhaps once in a year he may stumble. Can you, or will you, judge him by that? No, rather judge him by that which he is always doing. You are always thinking. Now that is your god which you are always thinking on. If on riches, then that is your god; or whatever it may be, that is your god. Examine then your heart by your thoughts; "for out of the abundance of the heart the mouth speaketh," (Matthew 12:34). Yes, for one word there is abundance of thoughts; for one good duty, there is abundance of thoughts. Therefore, if you will examine your heart, examine your thoughts.

Fourth, thoughts are the univocal acts of the heart, such as in which the heart shows its own nature. For example, the univocal act of light is to give light to the room. Now you cannot judge of the light by the heat, so well as by the shining. So an ill savor must be judged of by the stench, which is the univocal act of it. It may cause many other effects, but this is the proper act by which it shows itself. So the thoughts of men are the univocal acts of their hearts. Therefore, in Scripture they are called "the way of the heart." Just as the heart is, so are the thoughts. If the heart is proud, so are the thoughts; just according to the nature of the heart, so are the thoughts.

Fifth, they are the swiftest acts of the heart. If I judge of a scholar, I will judge him by that which he does *ex tempore*. If a fool studies, he may speak to purpose; but what a man does by his own inclination, that reveals what he is. Thoughts are the *extempore* acts of the heart. If your heart is heavenly, it will scatter *out* heavenly meditations; if carnal, then your thoughts are carnal. Thoughts are like visions in the night. Here we use this proverb: "his thoughts are gone a-suturing." If they are the swiftest acts of men's hearts, then they are most fit to express the nature of the heart.

Sixth, thoughts are the peculiar acts of the heart, peculiar to God only. The world may see what your outward life is, but your thoughts God alone sees. Neither angel, devil, nor man can see them. And as they are peculiar to God's eye, so He most regards what men's thoughts are. Therefore, the best way for a man to judge himself is to judge himself that way which God does— even by his thoughts. "The LORD knoweth the thoughts of man, that they are vanity," (Psalm 94:11). Examine yourselves in this then, concerning your thoughts, whether they are transformed or not. A man may say he has good thoughts of God, but let him examine whether it is so.

Seventh, thoughts are the *conscional* acts of the heart; *they are the greatest accusers or excusers of the heart.* They are, so to speak, the conscience's nose. It is true, the words of the tongue and the actions of the hands are all in the light and sight of the conscience; but the nearer a thing is to the conscience, the more able it is to judge of the conscience. Therefore, Paul puts the accusing or excusing especially on the thoughts: "Which shew the work of the law written in their hearts, their conscience also bearing witness, and their thoughts the mean while accusing or else excusing one another," (Romans 2:15).

We grant, a wicked man may have good thoughts, but they are thoughts descending, not ascending; they are cast into the heart by God, not raised out of the heart. "And when he was full forty years old, it came into his heart to visit his brethren the children of Israel," (Acts 7:23). Good thoughts grow *out* of the heart of the godly; they come from the bottom of it. A wicked man may have good thoughts cast into his mind, but he will fling them out again.

Second, we grant wicked men may have good thoughts, but examine whether they close with the heart or not. All the proper thoughts of a man are the possessions of the heart: "My days are past, my purposes are broken off, even the thoughts of my heart," (Job 17:11). They take hold of the heart, and they are at home in the heart. Here then examine your heart, whether the thoughts of God close with your heart. Does repentance close with your heart? Do you think of death, and do the thoughts thereof make you die daily? Or do you think of death, and yet not love to be held by that thought? Do you think of hell, and will you not be held by that thought of hell, but your thoughts are on your pleasures? So then, if your thoughts do not close with your heart, it is nothing to the purpose.

Third, there may be good thoughts in your heart, but it is questionable whether they are good or not if they come out of due season. If a printer prints never so well, and makes never so good letters, yet if he places one word where another should stand, he mars the whole document. So, good thoughts, if they are seasonable and in their proper place, they are the *effects* of the Spirit; but if out of season, they may be the thoughts of reprobates. For example, if you are at prayer, and then to be thinking of a sermon, it is nothing to the purpose. They must be seasonable, and bring forth fruit *in due season*: "And he shall be like a tree planted by the rivers of water, that bringeth forth his fruit in his season; his leaf also shall not wither; and whatsoever he doeth shall prosper," (Psalm 1:3). When you are at prayer, your thoughts must be suitable *to prayer*; for if your thoughts are never so good, yet if they are not seasonable and suitable to the action you have in hand, they are not actions of grace; grace cannot *accept* them.

Fourth, you may have good thoughts in your heart, but the question is whether they are counseled thoughts, such as you have determined to think on. "Therefore judge nothing before the time, until the Lord come, who both will bring to light the hidden things of darkness, and will make manifest the counsels of the hearts," (1 Corinthians 4:5). It may be you stumble on a good thought now and then; it may be when you are swearing you will say, "God forgive me"; when you have been drinking all the day, it may be a good thought steps in and cries, "God mercy"; but you do not go to school to learn the art of meditation, the science of holy thinking, or to say with David, "O God, my heart is fixed," (Psalm 108:1).

[Use 1] Now, if sin in thought is so great a sin, this should teach us what a horrible sin it is to sin in *deed*. Therefore, if thoughts are the smallest sins, and the Psalmist makes it an argument of God's quick-sighted power to see thoughts, "Thou understandest my thought afar off," (Psalm 139:2)—you will say that man is quick-sighted who can see a pin's head a hundred miles off—even so God sees thoughts. If a pin's point can stab a man, then a sword can much more. Now if thoughts are so heinous and capital a sin, how fearful a sin is it to commit sin in deed? For you to swear, to lie, to commit adultery, to keep wicked company, to mock at God's people, to live in covetousness—this is to commit sin in deed. If small sins are so damnable, what then are the greatest? If the cockatrice in the egg is such poison, what will it be when it is hatched? Sins in thought are imperfect, but outward actions are perfect.

It is a wicked distinction to say that some sins are *contra legem* (against the law) or *praeter legem* (beside the law). For *all* sins are against the law. "Then when lust hath conceived, it bringeth forth sin: and sin, when it is finished, bringeth forth death," (James 1:15). You that are a drunkard, your sin is finished; you are a true sinner in deed, if you live in the execution of any outward sin.

Again, sins in thought are *simple* sins; but sins in deed are compounded. Sin in thought is part of sin, but when it is in *deed*, it may be the cause of a thousand sins. For a man to think too much of his belly is a sin; but for a man to be drunken, this is abundance of sins—for it is an abuse of God's creatures, a spending of his substance, a weakening of his parts, a scandal to others, *etc*. Sin in deed is a sin with an addition. Sin in deed is an impudent sin. "I have spread out my hands all the day unto a rebellious people, which walketh in a way that was not good, after their own thoughts; A people that provoketh me to anger continually to my face; that sacrificeth in gardens, and burneth incense upon altars of brick," (Isaiah 65:2–3). That man is impudent indeed who will commit sin in deed, for he is neither ashamed of God's nor man's presence. If any man is a desperate sinner, this is he.

[Objection.] But it may be objected, how then can thoughts be said to be such sins, even sins of the highest part of a man?

[Solution.] I answer: A thief or rogue has burned a man's dwelling house, yet he may proceed further and burn his stable too. A thousand pounds and a shilling are more than a thousand pounds. Sins in thought are included within sins in deed. The soul's part of sin is the greatest part of sin. Now thoughts are the soul's part of sin. Yet sins in deed must needs be worse in regard of the progress of sin, and also because thoughts are included in them. Thoughts and deeds are more than thoughts alone.

[Use 2] I exhort and desire you therefore to consider.

[1] First, what great reason you have to set your thoughts on God. God Himself has merited this duty at your hands. "Many, O LORD my God, are thy wonderful works which thou hast done, and thy thoughts which are to us-ward: they cannot be reckoned up in order unto thee: if I would declare and speak of them, they are more than can be numbered," (Psalm 40:5). The Lord thinks on us from the cradle to the cross. If the Lord should have intermitted His thoughts of you, you could

not have subsisted. When you were up, the Lord thought how to feed you; when you were in bed, He thought how to preserve you. He does not think of you at one time and not at another, but He thinks on you when you are sick and when you are in health, asleep or awake; otherwise the devil would seize on you. "But I am poor and needy; yet the Lord thinketh upon me," (Psalm 40:17). And Nehemiah prayed, "Think upon me, my God, for good," (Nehemiah 13:31). Shall we call to God to think on us? Then surely it is our duty to think on Him. Yes, and He may justly call us to that duty.

[2] Secondly, consider with yourselves what thoughts they are which God calls for. "My son, give me thine heart," (Proverbs 23:26). He would gladly have your heart. He allows you to labor with your hands for your living, He allows you to use your feet to walk, and the rest of your members for their several purposes; but the Lord requires your heart. Therefore, give Him the thoughts of your heart. For if your neighbor comes to you for fire, you cannot give him fire if you take away the heat of it. So give the Lord your heart, and the thoughts of it will follow.

The devil *also* calls for your heart. Therefore, reason as Joseph did when he was tempted: "How then can I do this great wickedness, and sin against God?" (Genesis 39:9). My master has delivered into my hands all that he has, you only excepted, and shall I take you? How can I do this? So the Lord has withheld nothing from you but your heart. "My son, give me thine heart,"

(Proverbs 23:26). Yet will you deny it to Him, with the thoughts of it?

Tell me, you that are rich: would it be any disparagement to you to be God's servants, to set your thoughts on God? True, the great men of this world think it some disparagement to think on these things. But I tell you, you that are a gentleman—if you have grace, it makes you more than a gentleman. Grace does not take away men's honor and riches; but if he is a knight, it makes him *more* than a knight. And as Paul said to Philemon, "For perhaps he therefore departed for a season, that thou shouldest receive him for ever; Not now as a servant, but above a servant, a brother beloved," (Philemon 15–16). He was a servant when he was carnal, but now being a Christian he is more than a servant. If you have grace, it is an addition to your riches—riches, and more than riches. Therefore, give your hearts to God, and it will be the better for you.

[3] Thirdly, the Lord has made your thoughts your jewels. Your thoughts are precious; the Lord keeps them under lock and key, He will not let any see them. If all men should observe a man and look into him, yet they cannot see his thoughts. No, God has locked them up and made them *your* jewel. Will you then cast them into the mire? Will you prefer hawks and hounds in your thoughts before God? Can you sit at dinner and not once think of God, but always on base profit? Why, your thoughts are your jewels.

Again, a wise man will be wary of the companions he keeps. Your thoughts are your only companions. You never go out or in, but your thoughts go along with you. For this cause Solomon would have us place the word of God in our thoughts: "When thou goest, it shall lead thee; when thou sleepest, it shall keep thee; and when thou awakest, it shall talk with thee," (Proverbs 6:22). "My substance was not hid from thee, when I was made in secret, and curiously wrought in the lowest parts of the earth. Thine eyes did see my substance, yet being unperfect; and in thy book all my members were written, which in continuance were fashioned, when as yet there was none of them," (Psalm 139:15–16). "When I awake, I am still with thee," (Psalm 139:18).

Men will be careful what meat they eat, because such meat as they eat, such is their blood; and as their blood is, so is their body. Now as the body feeds on meat, so does the soul on thoughts. If we do not look to our thoughts, they will be subject to abundance of corruptions. "But I say unto you, That every idle word that men shall speak, they shall give account thereof in the day of judgment," (Matthew 12:36). And thoughts are the inward words of the heart. Now if men must give account of *every* idle word, then of *every* idle thought *also*.

Let this then teach all and every one of us, in the fear of God, to consider our thoughts, else our end will be destruction.

Sermon 2:
A Sermon of Self-Denial

Luke 9:23, "And he said unto them all, If any man will come after me, let him deny himself, and take up his cross daily, and follow me."

This text contains the first action required of every Christian, namely, *to deny himself*; concerning which observe:

First, the grounds of it.
Secondly, the reasons of it.
Thirdly, the occasion of it.
Fourthly, the parts of it.
Fifthly and lastly, the necessity of it.

I intend to handle these words as they are in relation to the context.

First, the grounds of this truth—that every man must deny himself. It is expressed here as twofold:

1. The contrariety between Christ and a man's self—"me, and himself." These two terms are contradictory to one another. "If any man will come after me, let him deny himself." These two cannot stand together.
2. The contrariety between self and self. If a man is in Christ, he has two selves: he has a self in himself, and a self out of himself. The self in himself is old Adam; the other in Christ, which is the new man. There is self-denying and self-

denied. If a man will find himself, he must lose himself. Paul must not be found in Paul having his own righteousness, but he must find himself in Christ. "Salvation belongeth unto the LORD," (Psalm 3:8). Therefore, let him deny himself.

Secondly, you may see its reason, which is threefold:

1. Christ's own example (verse 22). "The Son of man must suffer... must be rejected." Christ Himself denied Himself. He might have commanded for Himself; He might have demanded credit, honor, or riches, yet though He had no wicked self, but good self, yet He denied Himself. Therefore, if we will go after Christ, we must do so too.
2. Here is Christ's merit. He has merited this duty. Christ did not humble Himself for Himself, but He did it for us. Therefore, we may well deny ourselves for Him. This is included in this word *And*: "And if I have done this for you, I would have you do the like for me."
3. Here is Christ's command also: "Let him deny himself." Christ enjoins this to all that will come after Him: let him deny himself.

Thirdly, observe the occasion, and that is threefold:

1. Peter's offense. When Christ had told Peter and the rest of His apostles how He must suffer, Peter was offended, saying, "Master, favor Thyself."

Like a servant who, out of love to himself, would be loath that his master should be troubled, because then he thinks he shall be troubled also. Oh, says Christ, are you offended at this? I tell you, neither you nor any other can come after me unless you deny yourselves: "If any man will come after me..."

2. As Peter was offended, so also were the rest of the apostles. "And they were exceeding sorry," (Matthew 17:23). They thought to have gained credit in the world, and riches, and worldly preferment; and now it grieved them to hear that they must have a suffering kind of trade of it. Therefore Christ said not only to Peter, but to them all, "If any man will..."

3. Likewise, as His apostles were offended, so Christ foresaw that all the world would be offended at this. For many would gladly have Christ and their self-will too. But Christ gives a watchword beforehand: "If any man will..."

Fourthly, the parts of it. The whole duty is this: "Let him deny himself." Chrysostom on the text says, not only deny himself, but in the original "deny away himself." Not only deny credit, *etc.*, but *abhor* it. If it cannot be had but with the loss of Christ, we must not only barely deny self-respects, but abhor them and trample them under our feet.

The parts of this duty are two:
1. Let him take up his cross.

2. Let him deny himself and follow me.

The first is opposed to self-favoring, the second to self-doing.

First, let him take up his cross; let him not favor himself. He must be content to part with self-means and maintenance, and self-ends too. He must be content to part with all these. He that will come after me must lose many good friends, and many a good bit and sweet morsel to the flesh. He that will come after me must not stand on these terms. Suppose a cross of disgrace comes; take it up and wear it as your crown. Yes, you must be willing to take a cross before it is offered; and when you have it, you must be willing to bear it.

Secondly, he must follow me too. One's self will do as one's self would have him, that is true; but you must follow me, not yourself. Look to me, and frame yourselves to walk in my steps; take up my cross, *etc.*

Lastly, here is the necessity of it. It is absolutely true, a man may go to hell if he is so minded; he may follow himself to hell. But if a man values his salvation, then here is a hypothetical necessity, a necessity with an "if."

1. If he means to come after me, he must take up his cross and deny himself.
2. If a man would save his life, he must lose it; if he will lose it, he shall save it. If a man will keep his old relation, he may; but if he will find credit and life in heaven, he must deny all self-respects.
3. If a man will gain himself, let him deny himself.

Sermon 2: A Sermon on Self-Denial

But some say, "How shall we live then? How shall I hold up my head?" These men would gladly have the gain of the world. But "what is a man advantaged, if he gain the whole world, and lose himself, or be cast away?" (Luke 9:25). If you stand upon these terms, if you can balk a commandment for self-respects, you may lose your souls. But if you will save your souls, thus you must do. Again, the text says, "For whosoever shall be ashamed of me and of my words, of him shall the Son of man be ashamed," (Luke 9:26). Therefore, if ever you expect that the Son of man should not be ashamed of you, deny yourselves.

Now for the exposition.

"Deny himself"—*there* is the difficulty. A man cannot deny himself (2 Timothy 2:13). For *affirmare* (to affirm) and *negare* (to deny) are contradictions. Therefore, something must be meant by *one's self*. Yet by one's self is not meant the devil, as Micarius would have it. Since man has sinned, says he, the devil is got into him, and is as near to him as himself; he is another self within his own self, another heart within his own heart. Therefore, if he will come after Christ, he must forsake the devil. Though this is true, yet this is not the meaning of the text.

But first, a man's *corrupt* will, wit, reason, and all a man's corrupt self must be put off. "That ye put off concerning the former conversation the old man, which is corrupt according to the deceitful lusts," (Ephesians 4:22). This is a man's *self*. That is, you must lay aside the man that you are; you must not be the same man if you will follow Christ; you must be a new self in Christ.

Second, here is not only meant a man's corrupt will, wit, reason, and affections, but also all men's lusts and corruptions—all sins that cleave so close as if they were himself. "Mortify therefore your members which are upon the earth; fornication, uncleanness, inordinate affection, evil concupiscence, and covetousness, which is idolatry," (Colossians 3:5). The apostle counts a man's lusts to be as close to him as his members. Until a man is brought home to Christ, he and his sins are all one. He must deny himself, that is, all his lusts.

Third, by self is not only meant a man's corrupt self as sin and iniquity, but also a man's good self in some respects. Not only sins, but also father, mother, children, friends, even life itself—all, if they hinder him from Christ. So far he must deny all these. Yes, even grace itself; for a man may make a god of grace, or of prayer, *etc.* A man, I say, must deny all these so far as they are stumblings and offenses in his way to hinder him from Christ.

But, says one, "My father will disinherit me. I must humor him; he cannot endure a Puritan. If I must live as you would have me, I shall never have foot of his land." So the servant says, "I have a profane master, and he will turn me out of doors if I am so precise." Yes, but what says Christ? If you will come after me, you must deny father and mother and all. Better that your father disinherit you than that Christ should reject you.

Therefore, you must deny all, and take up His cross and make it your own.

And so, I come to the words, "Let him deny himself." Because justification is after regeneration, it is necessary to show what self-seeking is before you understand what self-denial is. By self-seeking I mean a man that has a *head lust* by which he is self-conceited of himself.

There are five things in self-seeking:
1. Self is a head lust.
2. It is a lust of self-conceit.
3. Of self-will.
4. Of self-wit.
5. Of self-confidence.

1. Self is a head lust; it is the main lust that keeps men from coming unto Christ. "For all seek their own, not the things which are Jesus Christ's," (Philippians 2:21). What is the reason? Because they seek self, they follow their own thoughts; and because they are ruled by their own selves, therefore they are not ruled by Christ.

That it is a head lust, I prove by five arguments.

1. Because it is the leading lust to all lusts; no lust in the world but self leads the dance. Why is a man proud? Because self would get credit. Why is a man covetous? Because self would have means and maintenance. Why is a man revengeful? Because self will not put up wrongs. Christ bids us, of all lusts, to take heed of self:

"And take heed to yourselves, lest at any time your hearts be overcharged with surfeiting, and drunkenness, and cares of this life, and so that day come upon you unawares," (Luke 21:34). Christ, knowing what a deceitful thing self is, bids us beware of self-beguiling. If we do not, self will bring us into many noisome lusts—surfeiting, drunkenness, the cares of this life, and so that day will come upon us unawares.

2. Self is the *cause* of all other lusts of the heart. It is the plotter and ruler of all; it is the master of arts. It was self that found out all lusts. *Self* found out pride, security, covetousness, and all other noisome lusts. *Self* is loath to take the pains that God would have it, and therefore *self* sets its wits on the hooked nail to secure everything. And it is here that Solomon says, "Lo, this only have I found, that God hath made man upright; but they have sought out many inventions," (Ecclesiastes 7:29). Man was upright, and God was the cause. He became wicked—how? Because *self* found out many inventions. Self is the inventor of all. And when self cannot get means enough by that way which God has allowed, then self seeks out for credit, wealth, pleasure, etc., devising ways of its own to gain reputation. In this way self is the cause of lust.

3. *Self* is an in-lust; it runs along through all the lusts of the flesh. There is in every lust of the flesh

an ounce of self. There would be no security in man, but that self would live at ease. So, as David said to the woman of Tekoah, "Is not the hand of Joab with thee in all this?" (2 Samuel 14:19), so may I say, has not self a hand in all this? Aquinas says it is called self out of an inordinate love that a man bears to himself and to those things which seem good to man's self. A man not only lusts after pride, pleasure, *etc.*, but he also looks to these things for self—either for some profit for self, or for credit for self. Self is always an in-lust. See it in the wicked steward: "And the lord commended the unjust steward, because he had done wisely," (Luke 16:8). He said within himself, "I cannot dig; to beg I am ashamed," (Luke 16:3). Self was too lazy to work, and too proud to beg; so he lessened his master's accounts for his own advantage, that others might receive him into their houses.

4. Self is a make-lust. A man would never break out into lust if it were not for self. "Lo, this is the man that made not God his strength; but trusted in the abundance of his riches, and strengthened himself in his wickedness," (Psalm 52:7). Doeg had a lust of confidence in his riches. This made Esau comfort himself against Jacob—he had a murderous lust to comfort himself (Genesis 27:42). The Jews had a lust of formality to pray, to hear, to bring offerings, to observe all the new

moons and ordinances of God. Yet they had no delight in these things; their minds were on their imaginations, and they loathed the Word of God. Why then would they do this? Because self was the cause. They thought thereby to stay themselves upon God: "For they call themselves of the holy city, and stay themselves upon the God of Israel; The LORD of hosts is his name," (Isaiah 48:2). And for this cause many among us come to church; this is a damnable lust.

Haman would not have boasted of being invited to the queen's banquet, except that the queen invited *none but himself* with the *king*. He would not have been so eager to answer Ahasuerus's question, but for himself. "Now Haman thought in his heart, To whom would the king delight to do honour more than to myself?" (Esther 6:6). *Self* makes a man covetous, injurious, and full of wrongs.

5. As it is a make-lust, so it is a requesting lust. Other lusts with some men are out of date. Many reprobates cannot endure drunkenness, nor pride, nor usury. These sins are out of date. Why does a man not love a miser? Because self is not the better for him; he cannot get so much as a dinner by him. Many other sins may be out of date with men, but self is never out of date; it is always in request. "Though while he lived he blessed his soul: and men will praise thee, when thou doest well to thyself," (Psalm 49:18). He has

none to make much of himself but himself. "Every man for himself, and God for us all," says self. But sometimes self is out of love—how? Because he will do no good but unto himself. This, men cannot endure; they say this is *self* out of his wits. But self, with the wisdom of the flesh, is always in request—that is, when men will be kind to others that they may be kind to them again. This self the world loves dearly.

6. Now I come to the second, which is self-conceit. Self-seeking presupposes self-conceitedness.

There is a bird called *starling*, a fair bird; in French it is called the Devil's bird. It is a blackbird, and yet it is conceited of itself that it is fair. By *starling* I mean first the conceit a man has of himself. "What, shall I," says self, "be disgraced by one that goes to plow and to cart, and shall I put it up? No, I am a gentleman," etc. Another says, "I am such and such a scholar, and shall I be contented with such a poor living?" These men will bear no reproof; "They would none of my counsel: they despised all my reproof. Therefore shall they eat of the fruit of their own way, and be filled with their own devices," (Proverbs 1:30–31).

Secondly, when a man is conceited of himself and of his own gifts—as commonly women are of their beauty, and scholars of their learning. A handsome man, and I warrant you he knows it. Diligent at church, and he knows it is so. And he thinks his case the *better* for it. Yes, you shall have men so conceited of their parts that they will even be conceited of their wicked parts, as Simon Magus was of his sorcery (Acts 8:9).

Thirdly, when a man is self-conceited of his actions. He does as Sisera's mother's ladies did, when they had given their verdict of Sisera's staying; they were immediately conceited of what a witty answer they made her (Judges 5:29–30). As if they should say, we have answered very wisely. So, a man cannot make a sermon but immediately he is conceited, "Oh, what a learned sermon it was." He cannot break a jest, but immediately he is conceited, "Oh, what a witty one it was." Yes, even of wicked actions. You will hear many an old man tell what pretty pranks (as he calls them) he played in his youth; and he tells it laughingly, which is a sign that he is self-conceited. Otherwise, surely, he would speak of it with shame and grief of heart.

Fourthly and lastly, self-conceit is when a man is self-conceited of the estate he is in. Many a man, though he is the child of hell, is nevertheless conceited that he *is* the child of God. Who, with the wretch in the Gospel, have conceits that they love God and Christ, and therefore with him they will come to the sacraments. But Christ will say to such as He did to him, "Friend, how camest thou in hither not having a wedding garment? And he was speechless. Then said the king to the servants, Bind him hand and foot, and take him away, and cast him into outer darkness; there shall be weeping and gnashing of teeth," (Matthew 22:12–13).

Sermon 2: A Sermon on Self-Denial

Can you conceive yourselves to be friends? Get you gone into utter darkness, that is, into hell, says our Saviour.

Now if you would know what self-conceit is, you must remember that it contains *four* things.

First, where there is self-conceit, there is no real worth at all. He that is self-conceited is a base man; take that for a rule. A self-conceited fellow is a base fellow, as we used to say. There is no real worth at all in a conceited man. All the worth that he has is either real as he thinks, or conceited. But what real worth can self have? You know what the Scripture says: "He hath shewed strength with his arm; he hath scattered the proud in the imagination of their hearts," (Luke 1:51). They may imagine that they are gentlemen, or that they have faith, and yet God scatters these men in their imaginations.

Secondly, as he has no real worth in himself, so he will not stand to the judgment of those that can judge him. God can tell the worth of everything, but they will not be judged by Him. God's ministers out of God's Word can tell him that he has no reason to think his case good; but he will not stand to the judgment of God's ministers. If a minister should come to a man and say to him, "Sir, you are conceited that you are a good Christian. I pray, what signs have you for it? You pray—so do reprobates. You hear the Word and receive the sacraments—so do reprobates. Have you no better signs than these? No better arguments than these? Why, I tell you, a reprobate has these and more than these too." A self-conceited man will be judged by none but himself. "The sluggard is wiser in his own conceit than seven men that can render a reason," (Proverbs 26:16). The sluggard is *loath* to take more pains. Why? He thinks he takes pains enough, and so he is conceited. More he will not do. Let seven men come and tell him that he must take more pains, yet he will not; because he is conceited that he does enough. Even so it is with the sluggish Christian. He is wise in his own conceit. For let seven ministers come and tell him that he must take more pains for heaven, or else he will never come there, yet he will not believe them. He thinks he is wiser than they; they are fools, as he imagines, though he has no reason so to think. He indeed is not as he should be, and God's ministers can bring reasons out of the Scriptures to prove it: "Wisdom is profitable to direct," (Ecclesiastes 10:10). But every conceited man is a blind man.

Thirdly, a self-conceited man, as he will not stand to the judgment of those that can judge him, so he has too high a conceit of himself. Be he never so little godly, he is immediately persuaded that he is a child of God. If a man has never so little humility or patience, if he comes to church, prays, or does but a few outward duties of religion, he thinks immediately it is a high wall to him, and that he shall go to heaven for sure. And let other men be never so holy, strict, religious, and pious in their ways, yet he is apt to think them reprobates. If he sees never so little slips among them, he is immediately ready to say they are all worthless. If any are false among them, he is ready to say they are all hounds. But if he is persuaded that he has never so little faith, oh, immediately he thinks *that* is a high wall.

Fourthly and lastly, he rests in the judgment of himself, and this is the case of thousands in the world. They think well of their own cases, that when they die they shall go to heaven—there is no question but Christ will save them—and from this conceit they will never be moved. Let all the ministers in the world come, one after another, and uncover to a wicked man his estate, yet he will not leave his own verdict. "Though thou shouldest bray a fool in a mortar among wheat with a pestle, yet will not his foolishness depart from him," (Proverbs 27:22). So, if you should beat these men with the threatenings of the law, with the plagues contained in the Bible, making their consciences black and blue (as we use to say), yet they will not leave off their conceitedness.

Now the reasons of this are four.

1. Because all sinners are fools. "The foolish shall not stand in thy sight: thou hatest all workers of iniquity," (Psalm 5:5). All that work iniquity are fools. A self-conceited fool is a proverb. And our Saviour, who knew the combination of all sins, joins pride and foolishness together: "Thefts, covetousness, wickedness, deceit, lasciviousness, an evil eye, blasphemy, pride, foolishness," (Mark 7:22). A proud, conceited man and a fool are put together by our Savior.

And this is the cause why so many thousands in the world are conceited of themselves, that their case is good when it is nothing so—because they are fools. None but fools will prefer trinkets before jewels, and temporary things before heavenly things. Yet such are the wise men of this world. That man is a fool that cannot eat his meat. And such is every sinner. His soul has no food but Christ, the Word, and His promises, yet he knows not how to feed on them. He has no covering to hide his nakedness but Christ, yet he knows not how to put on Christ. Therefore, he is a fool.

2. Men are *born* fools. Of all fools, none so self-conceited as the born fool. One that has been a wise man knows how to hold his peace, but a born fool is invincible. "For vain man would be wise, though man be born like a wild ass's colt," (Job 11:12). Of all creatures, the foal of the ass is the simplest; then the wild ass's colt must be most simple. So, although a man is born a fool, yet he would be counted wise. He is conceited that all the ministers in the world cannot direct him. No, he is wise enough for that matter. This folly is bred and born in him. He has it by nature, and that is the reason it is hardly scraped off. They are ready to say they are as wise as the ministers themselves.

Sermon 2: A Sermon on Self-Denial

I call not into question the wit of many. I know many of you are understanding men and women. But I speak now of the wisdom of the Spirit, and how you may understand to save your souls. What is it for a man to be worldly wise, to get riches and honor, and to behave himself like a gentleman, and yet be a fool in seeking his salvation? This is to be penny-wise, but here is the question: are you not pound-foolish? Can you go on in your sins—swearing, etc.? Then surely you are pound-foolish. All your wisdom and money avail nothing. Alas, you are but penny gentlemen. The Sodomites in Genesis 19 were blind; they could not find the door. They could see well enough otherwise, they were only blind in this. So man is *stultus ad hoc (foolish in this respect)*. He is wise enough for anything in the world but this. Take him for husbandry, and his knowledge is good. For matters of behavior, he can carry himself as well as the wisest. He is only *stultus ad hoc—for salvation he is a fool*, a born fool, and self-conceited.

3. Men are self-conceited about their own estate. Those that praise themselves, we use to say, have ill neighbors. So, if a fool had a good neighbor to tell him of his folly, and to laugh at him for it, he would not praise himself. So, he that praises himself, it is certain he has ill neighbors. The reason men are well-conceited of themselves is because they have ill neighbors. They think they are honest, and so do their neighbors. But if a drunkard could go nowhere without everyone

telling him he was a hellhound, he would not be drunk. But an ill neighbor tells him he need not fear, by the grace of God he shall do well enough, he is a good Christian. And therefore it is that when fools are not answered according to their folly, they are conceited of themselves. When men are flattered, others think well of them, and so they also think their own case good. For they say, "If I were not a good Christian, such and such would not be acquainted with me."

4. Because the Lord delivers many up to the spirit of slumber. "According as it is written, God hath given them the spirit of slumber, eyes that they should not see, and ears that they should not hear," (Romans 11:8). The *black poppy seed* will cast a man into such a sleep as that his eyes shall be wide open and yet he cannot see. So, the Lord has cast men into a slumber like a man between sleeping and waking. Of all sleep, none is like slumber, because it is full of imaginations. Never is a man so full of dreams as when he is in a slumber. If a man were a drunkard and sunk deep in all evil, and lulled in the sea of security, he could not be so well-conceited. But now that his eyes are half open, half shut; half awake, half asleep; half out, half in, he thinks his repentance is good, his case good, and he hopes he shall find mercy at the hands of God as well as the best Puritan in the parish. They are like the dreamer

(as Joseph's brethren called him), singular—in Hebrew, "the master dreamer." They dream they shall have mercy and not be damned. These men are in a slumber; they have eyes and see not, ears and hear not. "Yet they also have erred through wine, and through strong drink are out of the way; the priest and the prophet have erred through strong drink, they are swallowed up of wine, they are out of the way through strong drink; they err in vision, they stumble in judgment," (Isaiah 28:7). They see the judgment of God, but they do not perceive it.

Consider what a woeful case these men are in, and how the Scripture calls this self-conceit.

First, it calls it nothing but a thought: "If a man think himself to be something, when he is nothing, he deceives himself," (Galatians 6:3). To think yourself a Christian is a vain thought.

Second, the Scripture calls it superstition. What a vain thing it is for a man to be supposing! They suppose they shall go to heaven. They suppose they are better than others, better than those on whom the tower in Siloam fell. And so many suppose they are not in the gall of bitterness nor in the bond of iniquity.

Third, it calls them shadows: "Surely every man walketh in a vain shew," (Psalm 39:6). That is, their repentance shows as if it were good repentance. They can speak lowly, there is a show that they are humble. Man walks in a vain show, like a tradesman who has an abundance of things which he makes a show of, yet none are his own. So, he talks of grace which was never his.

Fourth, it calls them imaginations (Acts 4).

Fifth, it calls them appearances (Matthew 6:16). So men appear at a sermon, but their hearts never bow down before the Word. They are nothing but appearances (1 Corinthians 3). In this way you may think yourselves, or suppose yourselves, to be in a good state, when it would be better that you appeared to be a hell-hound than a Christian, and not be one indeed. For then there would be some hope that you would seek help. If a man is sick but seems to be well, none will look after him as they would if he seemed sick indeed; and therefore this is the most dangerous sickness. So if men did seem to be damned wretches—that they were born and continue in sin, and when they die they must be damned—if men feared this, they would look out for help.

Second, consider that, as long as you are well-conceited of yourself, Christ has *no* commission to call you. And Christ will do nothing but what he has commission to do; he will not run into a *praemunire* (to act without lawful authority). Christ testifies to all the world that he has no commission from his Father for such: "I am not come to call the righteous, but sinners to repentance," (Matthew 9:13)—that is, those that are righteous in their own esteem and thoughts, but are not. If a man tells them they are fitter for hell than for heaven, they are better-conceited of themselves than to believe it. If a man tells them that, for all their profession, they may be hell-hounds, yet they think better of their profession than that. Consider then what a case you are in, if you are outside Christ's way.

Third, as Christ has no commission, so he is glad he has not, and he gives thanks to his Father that he was not given such a commission. "In that hour Jesus rejoiced in spirit, and said, I thank thee, O Father... that thou hast hid these things from the wise and prudent, and hast revealed them unto babes," (Luke 10:21). As if he said, "You do not convert those that are self-conceited, those that think they shall not be damned, those that suppose they need no summons because they are righteous enough. Father, I am glad of it." And it is said there that Jesus rejoiced. He rejoices that he is sent to poor souls, such as are the offscouring of the world. But he that is self-conceited thinks he is wiser than that. Christ tells him he must take up the cross, but he thinks he has more wit, that he can go a wiser way, that he has an easier path to heaven, that he will not have the cross. And I tell you, then Christ will not have you, but will be glad to see you damned.

Fourth and lastly, he who is self-conceited is in the broad way to hell. There are many ways to hell: the covetous goes one way, the drunkard goes another, there are a thousand ways to hell. Yet though there are sundry ways, they all meet in self-conceit. That is the broad highway where all meet. Self-conceit is not only a way to hell, it is the broad way where all ways meet. "There is a way which seemeth right unto a man, but the end thereof are the ways of death," (Proverbs 14:12). There is the wage, there all the ways meet. Oh then, examine yourselves. I should give you signs and tokens to make it appear unto you, but time will not allow.

Sermon 3:
The Efficacy of Importunate Prayer Part 1

Luke 11:9, "Ask, and it shall be given you; seek, and ye shall find; knock, and it shall be opened unto you."

Our Savior Christ, being asked by one of his disciples how they should pray, here teaches them two things. First, a pattern of prayer, in the second, third, and fourth verses; Say, "Our Father," etc. (Luke 11:2–4). Secondly, he teaches them the importunity of prayer, which he sets forth by the parable of a man who, having a guest come to him at midnight and having nothing to set before him, went to his friend to beg him to lend three loaves.

At first he simply begs, "Lend me three loaves." The door is shut, says his friend, and I cannot open it now. Secondly, he begins to entreat and beseech him to do him this favor: "He had a guest come to him, and he knew not what to do: Why, 'tis midnight, says he, is there no other time to come but now?" Thirdly, he begins to knock; he must needs have them, though it be an unreasonable hour. "Why, I tell you I am in bed." Then he entreats him as a friend. "Friend, lend me;" "Be a friend to me, I need a loaf," he says again. Yet the man would not leave knocking: at last, with much *ado*, the man rises, saying, "Will ye not be answered?," and he lends him three loaves, because of his importunity. Now, says our

Saviour, I say unto you, though he would not give him as a friend, yet because of his importunity he will. The parable is this: you are that man, O Christian soul; this guest is your own self; now come home to yourself like the Prodigal, who, when he came to himself, goes to his father and friend. This friend is Christ, whom you are to pray to; these three loaves are grace, mercy, and peace, these you are to pray for. It may be Christ answers you in your conscience, "It is midnight, thou comest too late; there is no mercy for thee." The soul prays still, "O Lord, awaken and help me." It may be the Lord will answer you by terror in your soul, "The door of mercy is shut; thou shouldst have come rather." Yet the soul cries, "Lord, open unto me": "No," says the Lord, "all my children have mercy already; now mercy is asleep; I have converted them already; they came in due season; thou comest at midnight; there is no mercy for such a hell-hound as thou art." "Up, Lord, have mercy on me," says the poor soul, "and look on me," *etc*. "Look on me," says the Lord; "I came to save the lost sheep of the house of Israel: there was a time when I would have converted thee, when I called unto thee early and late: but now I am asleep, and my mercy is asleep; it hath been awake as long as it could well hold open its eyes; and comest thou now?" Oh, the soul cries still and will never give over: if mercy is to be had at the throne of grace, he will have it. Even as a beggar being at a gentleman's door, they bid him be gone, "There is nothing to be had." "No," says the beggar, "I will not be gone; here is something to be had, and I will have something, or else I will die at the door." The gentleman, hearing him say so, thinks it would be a shame for him if he should die at his door, and gives him something. So, when the soul is in this way importunate, because of importunity it shall be granted. Truly I say to you, if you will ask in this way, it shall be given you. These words contain in them the main duty of importunate prayer: ask; if asking will not serve, seek; if seeking will not serve, then knock; try *all* means.

Another parable our Savior puts forth (Luke 18:1–8), that men ought always to pray and not to faint. There was a poor widow wronged by her adversary, and there was no judge to right her but an unjust one, so that she had but poor hopes; yet she resolves to go, or else she shall be undone; therefore, if she perish, she will perish at his feet. He calls her all to nought. "Oh, for God's sake, help me," says she. "I care not for God nor man," says the judge. "Nay, good my Lord," says the woman. The judge, seeing her thus importunate, said, "I shall be troubled with her if I do her not justice." How much more, says the text, shall not God avenge his elect, which cry day and night unto him? (Luke 18:1–7).

Objector: But some man may demand, What is importunate prayer?

Answer: I answer, it is a restless prayer which will take no "no," nor contumelious repulse, but is, in a holy manner, impudent until it is given. There are in it *four things:*

First, it is *restless*: he that is importunate cannot rest until he prospers in his suit before God. As the poor woman of Canaan, she sought the Lord God of heaven and earth—she was of the cursed stock of Ham whom the Lord commanded Israel to destroy; yet she repented and became of the faith of Abraham—to see if the Lord would own her. But the Lord seemed to reject her and suffered the devil to possess her daughter. Now, might not this poor woman think she had made a sorry change of religion, seeing that God, the author of it, would not own her but suffered the devil to possess her daughter? But see the importunity of this woman, she would not be quiet until she had found Christ (Mark 7:24–25). Christ could not be hid. No? What, could he not hide himself in some corner? No, no, she thinks, there is a Christ, and if he is to be had under the canopy of heaven, *I will have him*. Even so it is with the soul that is importunate in prayer, it is *restless*. What if Christ does hide himself in the Word and will not own a poor soul; yet the poor soul knows there is a Christ, and if he is to be found in the whole world, he will have him. "I will," says he, "turn over all duties; I will go to all the ministers that are near; I will use all the means." Now Christ cannot be hid from such a soul that is in this way importunate. Now, as it is a prayer that will take no "no," so first it will take no privative "no" of silence; secondly, no positive "no" of denial.

First, it will take *no* negative answer of silence. A man that is importunate in prayer must and will have some answer. He is not like Baal's priests, who could get no answer (1 Kings 18:26), nor like wicked men that pray in their pews, not knowing what they say, nor whether God hears them. An importunate prayer will have an answer, like the woman of Canaan: "Have mercy on me, O Lord," she said. But Christ answered not a word. Was she done then? No, she cried all the more, "Have mercy on me, O Lord." She was so importunate that his disciples were ashamed to hear her. Yet she cried, "Have mercy on my daughter; the devil has my daughter, and misery will have me unless you have mercy on us." Christ answered her not a word. It was much trouble to her to have her daughter vexed with a devil, but this troubled her much more—that Christ, in whom all her hope rested, would not hear her nor give her one look. Might she not think, "Is this the merciful Savior, so full of pity and compassion? Is this he who made proclamation to all the world, saying, 'Come unto me, all ye that labour and are heavy laden, and I will give you rest,' (Matthew 11:28)? And I am wearied by reason of the devil that possesses my daughter, yet he regards me not." In this way she might have thought. Yet these discouragements could not put her off, but she cried all the more, until the apostles were ashamed that Christ would let her stand there so. Yet she stood it out and prevailed.

Second, it will take *no denial*. When she had an answer, and that flat against her, it was like bellows to the fire—she was so much the more inflamed. She doubled her efforts: "Have mercy on me, O Lord." Christ put her off with a denial: "I am not sent but unto the lost sheep of the house of Israel," (Matthew 15:24). "I come for sheep, not goats. You are of the Canaanites, upon whom I have set a brand of damnation, a servant of servants, a slave of hell and darkness. These are your people and your blood, but I come to save those of the house of Israel." But the denial of an importunate soul is like a dam across a river—the more it is stopped, the more violently it presses on. So this poor woman became *all the more* eager with Christ. She had cried before, but now she worshipped him: "Then came she and worshipped him, saying, Lord, help me," (Matthew 15:25). As if she said, "Lord, help me now. I am one of your lost sheep. I confess I am a Canaanite, I am of that damned blood, yet Lord help me. I am persuaded that you can take a course to help me. You can cast some mercy even on a Canaanite." In this way you see, an importunate soul will take no denial, but will renew its forces at the throne of grace.

Third, an importunate prayer will take no reproachful repulse. Suppose God should answer never a syllable to your prayer—yet you will pray. Suppose he does answer, and that against you—yet still you will pray. No, suppose he calls you all to nothing, making your conscience remember your sins and abominations, making you think heaven is shut against you and God has shut his ears, calling you "dog," "hell-hound," "wretch," and the like—yet nothing can break you off *if* you are truly importunate. So this woman was not driven off by Christ sending the devil into her daughter, nor by Christ hiding himself when she sought him, nor by Christ answering never a word, nor by the disciples' rebukes, nor by his denial, nor by his reproach—for he called her a dog: "It is not meet to take the children's bread, and to cast it to dogs," (Matthew 15:26). What creature but an importunate one could have gone so far? But see here the nature of importunity—it gets *within* Christ and takes advantage. She confessed the charge: "Truth, Lord: yet the dogs eat of the crumbs which fall from their masters' table," (Matthew 15:27). She said, "You have spoken rightly, Lord, I am a dog, a wicked woman. Yet let me have the privileges that dogs have. Though dogs may not be equal with children at the table, yet they may wait under the table. I acknowledge that your children are so plentifully fed that crumbs fall from the table; therefore let me have the privilege of a dog. Naaman the Syrian was a dog as well as I. Rahab the harlot was a dog as well as I. Ruth was counted a dog as well as I. Yet these received crumbs. Truth, Lord, I am a dog, yet your mercy can transform a dog. Of these stones you are able to raise up children unto Abraham," (Matthew 3:9). It is in this way with an importunate soul; though God call it vile, and cast reproachful terms upon it—saying in effect, "I would as soon accept swine's blood as hear you"—yet if you are importunate, you will bear any reproach.

Fourth, an importunate prayer is bold, yet in a holy manner. As an impudent beggar who is needy counts it no breach of manners to keep begging even when bidden to be silent, or as a poor petitioner before the king who will not be quiet though the king bids him hold his peace, but still cries, "Help me, Lord, O King!" So, the Canaanite woman's prayer was bold to the point of seeming impudence, yet it was holy.

I remember a story of a poor woman in Essex condemned to die. She began crying and screeching, as if to pierce heaven itself. The judge and the bench commanded her to be silent. "O my lord," said she, "it is for my life that I beg. I beseech you, it is for my life." So, when a soul comes before God and begs for mercy, it must remember it is *for its life*. "O Lord, it is for my life." Now though the Lord may not answer, and though he may let the soul go about with a heavy heart, yet if the soul cries out, "It is for my life—if I must go to hell, I will go to hell from the throne of grace, weeping and wailing for my sins, catching hold on the horns of the altar"—this soul shall find mercy.

I have marveled at the narrative in Luke 5—it is a strange passage where this holy kind of boldness was seen. Our Savior was preaching in a house to the people, and there was a poor man who could not come near him. So his friends lifted him to the rooftop, untiled it, and let him down. The debris could not help but fall on Christ's head or on his hearers. Was this not an impudent act? Could they not have waited until the sermon was over?

But importunity *knows no manners*. Though they interrupted Christ, he did not rebuke them, but said, "Man, thy sins are forgiven thee," (Luke 5:20).

Therefore, let us come *boldly* to the throne of grace (Hebrews 4:16). Not as if God had given leave to be *irreverent*, but as to a generous and loving man of whom we say, "He is so kind, you may say anything to him. Come to him at dinner, and he will rise up and hear you. Whatever business he is about, yet he will hear you." Even so it is with God: he is such a God that poor souls may be bold before him to lay open their case and show their condition. Now when souls come with this holy boldness, giving the Lord no rest until he establishes them (Isaiah 62:7), then God says, "How now? Can I not be at rest for you?" This holy kind of boldness in prayer will *give the Lord no rest*.

The reasons why we must seek importunately are *three*.

First, in regard to God's majesty. He loves to be sought to, and it is fitting that he should be. Among men, we call it pride when someone loves to be much entreated; and we say of such a one, "He loves to be asked." This is a fault among men, because men are bound to do good. Yet the Lord is not bound to us. If we sin, he is not bound to pardon us. The Lord, being a God of majesty, expects to be sought unto for his mercy, and he requires that we be importunate. In this way he says, "I will put my Spirit within you, and cause you to walk in my statutes... I will also yet for this be enquired of by the house of Israel, to do it for them," (Ezekiel 36:27, 37). Suppose a man needs a thousand dollars. Will the gentleman give it freely without security? No, he says, "I will have good security for it." So when we come for such high mercies as these—for such infinite compassions—God requires that we seek him earnestly for them. And Christ, the Son of God, is the great heir; those who are debtors to him must be importunate with him if they would have peace with him.

If one would marry a rich heir, possessing all the dignity the land can afford, he expects to be well sought after. So the Lord Jesus, heir of the whole world, if you would be joined to him, you must seek him earnestly. He looks for prayer, for he loves to hear his children cry. This is one of his titles: though he is God, yet he is the hearer of prayer (Psalm 65:2).

Again, we have wronged his Majesty. Suppose your servant wrongs you—you may say you will pardon him, but first you will make him humble himself before you. He shall, and must, know that he has wronged a good master. So God is willing to pardon you, but he will make your very soul know that you have sinned against a good God. He will make it appear by your prayer. He will make your spirit melt, he will fill your face with shame and confusion, he will make you know what a patient God you have rebelled against. Otherwise, the Lord will never pardon you. Do you think to pacify God with a lazy prayer—with coming to church and saying,

"Have mercy upon me, most merciful Father"? Do you think the Lord will have mercy on you for that? No, no. He may send you quickly to hell for all that. He will make you cry and cry again with groans. He will make you cry out and pray in another manner altogether, and he will make the sovereignty of his mercy to be seen in your salvation. Therefore, in regard to God's majesty, he loves men to be importunate.

Second, in regard to God's mercy. It is a disgrace to mercy to be begged coldly. It is a dishonor to God's bounty for a man to beg it with lukewarm importunity. What do you think of the mercy of God? Do you imagine it is not worth a groan, not worth more than the rattling off of a *Paternoster*? Do you make God's mercy of such base esteem? This is a disgrace to God's goodness, to be so cold or lifeless in prayer. "Thou hast not called upon me, O Jacob; but thou hast been weary of me, O Israel. Thou hast not honoured me with thy sacrifices," (Isaiah 43:22–23). You have too short a breath in your prayers, you care not how soon you come to an end. Do you bring lazy prayers and lay them upon my altar? You have not honored me.

Among the Romans, when any man was condemned to die, if he sought mercy, he was to bring his father and mother and all his kin and friends with him. They came with tears on their faces, with torn garments, kneeling down, crying mightily before the judge—and then they thought justice was honored. In this way they honored justice among men for one condemned to die. And so the Lord loves that his mercy should be honored. Therefore, he will have prayer to be importunate, so that by our groans it may appear how highly we esteem grace. Our souls must pant and gasp after grace. The Spirit of the Lord is the very breath of our souls, and our hearts will die without it. This is the honor of mercy, and therefore the Lord will have us be importunate.

Third, importunity must be, in regard to ourselves, else we cannot truly value mercy. Soon come, soon gone; lightly gotten, quickly forgotten. "I have it, let us be merry and spend it; when this is gone, I know where to get more." But if a man had labored hard for it, and must labor for more if he is to have more, then he would value it better. The world esteems mercy lightly—why? The greatest misers are often those who were once poor. When a poor man has gained riches, he is more covetous than the one born to wealth. The one who comes lightly by it spends freely, while the other craves it greedily because he remembers what it cost. So, the Lord loves that we should come hardly by mercy—not that he sells it for our pains, but for our good. We are not otherwise capable of it. "They shall come with weeping, and with supplications will I lead them," (Jeremiah 31:9). This is a beautiful phrase: God leads a soul up and down with supplications before granting its request, just as a beggar on the road follows after a gentleman. The gentleman passes by as if he does not notice, but the beggar keeps crying, "For God's sake, sir, bestow something on me." The gentleman goes on, until at last he reaches his house, and then he grants the request. Even so, God leads a soul from one duty to another until it has come to the place he intends, and then he hears and says, "What is your petition? I will pardon you."

But why is it, someone may ask, that *so few* are importunate in prayer?

I answer, first, because men count prayer a penance. There is a natural kind of popery in men's hearts. The papists, when men sin, make them perform penance—pilgrimages, scourging, so many *Paternosters* and *Ave Marias*—where prayer is *reckoned* as a punishment. This natural popery is in men's hearts still. They count prayer laborious, they are weary of it. They are not eager for it. They do not look upon prayer as a blessing, but as a burden. "Ye said also, Behold, what a weariness is it!" (Malachi 1:13). They were weary of God's service. "Oh," they say, "that the minister would soon have done!" They would rather be in the alehouse or about their business. All good duties are penance to the carnal man. And if a man must do penance, he will do as little as possible. The rogue cares not for too much whipping.

Men are content with formality. Many pray as Haman spoke the king's words before Mordecai—he would rather have led him to the gallows, yet he said, "Thus shall it be done to the man whom the king delighteth to honour," (Esther 6:11), because he dared not refuse. It was mere form. And so men go to church, hear the Word, pray, and receive sacraments for form's sake, or because it is the fashion. They think if they do not, they cannot be saved.

You may hear the drunkard say, "I am sorry for my drunkenness"—but he lies, for the next day he is at the alehouse again. The whoremonger says, "Lord, I am sorry I sinned against you"—but he lies, for the next woman he meets, he falls to whoring again. The covetous man says, "I am sorry for my worldly thoughts"—but he lies, for he spends all day carking and caring, with a thousand vain projects in his head. They only say prayers, they do not pray. I do not deny saying prayers, if they truly pray. Our Savior said, "When ye pray, say, Our Father," (Luke 11:2). But the proud man dishonors God's name, saying, "Thy will be done," when he is not humble and zealous, as God's will requires. He says, "Forgive us our trespasses," but he does not pray it, for he wrongs his neighbor and refuses to forgive. He says, "Lead us not into temptation," but he does not pray it, for he runs straight into temptation. And this is why men are not importunate—because their prayers are mere form.

Third, because they are gentleman-beggars. Of all beggars, none is prouder than the gentleman-beggar. Tell him he has lived wastefully, he puts his hands on his hips and says, "I am not as every beggar. I am well-born, descended from good stock." His heart will not stoop. So men are gentleman-beggars before God. "We were born of Christian parents," they say. "We were baptized as children of God already. What, are only Puritans the children of God? We are descended as well as the best." These are proud, and not yet sensible of their misery.

When John preached to and baptized the scribes and Pharisees, he called them out plainly: "O generation of vipers, who hath warned you to flee from the wrath to come?" (Matthew 3:7). "Viper?" they said. "Viper in your teeth! We are children of Abraham. Do you call us vipers? If you say so, then we must cry, 'We are damned!' and we would have need of mercy." In this sense, men are gentleman-beggars.

Another reason men are not importunate is their wrong ideas of prayer.

First, they have high thoughts of their *own* prayers. They mutter half-asleep between pillow and blanket in the morning, and think they have done God good service, so that he cannot damn them. At night they say, "Lord, have mercy on me," and then sleep soundly, thinking God must keep them till morning. At meals they say, "Lord, bless this food," and then fall to eating, believing God must sanctify it. They think much babbling will gain them a hearing (Matthew 6:7). But if poor souls knew how unseemly and unfit their prayers were, how lacking in true knowledge of their estate, they would cry, "Is this prayer for my soul, for such infinite mercy? Lord, how do I abuse your throne of grace, your sabbaths, your house, your name, and all your ordinances!" The importunate soul is ashamed of its prayers, while these are insolent. Their prayers are damned, and so are they.

Second, as men think highly of their prayers, they think little of their sins. They do not see their sins as they are. They are like Abner, who said, "Let the young men now arise, and play before us," (2 Samuel 2:14). They make sport of bloodshed. They strum on instruments and think it little worse than David playing on his harp (Amos 6:5). If they commit adultery, they say it is but a trick of youth. If they lie, it is only when cornered. But the man who does not feel his sins as David did, until his heart aches for them, will never find favor with God.

Third, as they think little of their sins, so they think little of God. They cannot believe God will damn a man for drinking a pot with his friend. "I cannot think God is so strict. No, I love God with all my heart," they say—and they think God is of their mind. They imagine God to be like themselves. "Thou thoughtest that I was altogether such an one as thyself," (Psalm 50:21). They say, "If I were God, I would not be so strict." They say, "God will not be angry forever," (Jeremiah 3:5). Suppose a man skips church, or speaks an unclean word—will God be angry for that? Suppose a man is negligent in duty—will God require every day's work? "Tush, God will not," they say (Psalm 10:13). And int his way they are not importunate.

Lastly, they have wrong thoughts of importunity *itself*. If a man knocks once, twice, or thrice, and no one answers, he goes away. That is ill manners. If you are importunate, you will knock seven times. Those within may say, "Be gone, hold your peace," but you will not accept that answer.

Beloved, men are close-handed—they are unwilling to give. And they are close-hearted too—they are unwilling to take the pains to ask of God. They dislike others being importunate with them, and so they dislike being importunate with God. Examine yourselves, then, in this duty. For importunate prayer is *always* the prayer of an importunate man.

Sermon 4:
The Efficacy of Importunate Prayer Part 2

The Second Sermon.

Luke 11:9, "Ask, and it shall be given you; seek, and ye shall find; knock, and it shall be opened unto you."

To proceed then: There are six signs to know whether our prayers are importunate or not.

First, importunate prayer is always the prayer of an importunate man. The man himself must be importunate if his prayer is to be so. But how can a man importune God for mercy when his very person calls upon God for vengeance? It must be the prayer of a godly heart. "Preserve my soul; for I am holy," (Psalm 86:2). David prayed, and he was holy when he prayed. His prayer testified that he labored after holiness. Therefore, when you go to God in prayer, consider whether you can say, "Lord, hear me, for I am holy, and I would gladly be more holy." But if saying such words chokes you, then your prayer condemns you.

In all begging, it is a great matter who it is that begs at the door. "Who is that?" asks the householder. If he opens and sees it is a thief, he says, "Oh, it is you. You may stand long enough; you shall never have alms of me." So it is with prayer—it is all in all who it is that prays.

The woman with the issue touched our Savior,

and when he asked who touched him, and saw the woman, he said, "Daughter, be of good comfort," (Luke 8:48). So, when a man prays to God, the Lord asks, "Who is that that seeks these mercies?" If the Lord sees it is a drunkard or a covetous man, he says, "Is it you? You may wait till Doomsday and never find mercy." The Spirit of supplication is called the Spirit of grace (Zechariah 12:10). If you do not have the Spirit of grace, you cannot pray. The text does not say, *whosoever asks the Father in my name*, but *whatsoever you ask the Father in my name*. Many may use the name of Christ at the throne of grace, but only those who are in Christ can truly pray. "If ye abide in me, and my words abide in you, ye shall ask what ye will, and it shall be done unto you," (John 15:7). If you do not walk in holiness, you cannot be an importunate orator like Moses the man of God. The prayer of a wicked man, as Augustine said, is *tanquam latratus canum—no better than the barking of dogs or the grunting of swine*. Therefore, you who know you live in sin—your prayers will never prevail at the throne of grace for eternal mercy.

Secondly, importunate prayer is the prayer of a pure conscience. Suppose a man does not see that he lives in sin, yet if his conscience cries guilty, if he has a foul conscience, his prayer will never prevail with God. "If I regard iniquity in my heart, the Lord will not hear me," (Psalm 66:18). If your conscience can tell you that you cherish iniquity, the Lord will not hear you. "I thank God, whom I serve from my forefathers with pure conscience," (2 Timothy 1:3). If a man prays with a conscience that tells him he regards sin, he shall not succeed. Many pray, for conscience will force them to pray, but they may pray until they go to hell, and still never be delivered, if they keep even one sin unrepented of.

I remember a story of a poor woman troubled in conscience. Many ministers visited her. At last, one came who, after much talk and prayer, touched upon one sin she was guilty of, and unwilling to part with. Then the woman cried out, "Until now you have spoken to the post, but now you have hit the mark. My conscience tells me I have been unwilling to part with this sin, but I must leave it or I cannot be saved." An evil conscience cannot have good hope. Even the pagans had this light, that the gods must be honored with purity. They wrote on the doors of their temples, "Let none with a guilty conscience enter here."

Thirdly, importunate prayer is full of strong arguments. Job said, "I would order my cause before him, and fill my mouth with arguments," (Job 23:4). So, an importunate man at the throne of grace will bring all arguments to persuade God. If he prays for some particular grace, he will press every reason he can find, "Lord, this is a grace of the covenant. Without it I am overcome by temptations. You have called me to be a minister—I cannot work upon men's consciences without it." A good orator before God must be a good logician. The high priests were to have Urim and

Thummim, which signified knowledge and perfection—two parts of logic. So must a minister be: a sound logician at the throne of grace.

Fourthly, importunate prayer is a stout prayer. "Continue in prayer, and watch in the same with thanksgiving," (Colossians 4:2). A weak-hearted prayer is cold, spiritless. Men have wit and strength enough for sin, but not for prayer. You cannot prevail with God unless you stand to it. Jacob prevailed by wrestling. Prayer is fighting, a holy violence. You cannot gain mercy from God unless you lay all your strength upon it. As a father who holds an apple in his hand, and his child would have it—he opens one finger, then another, until at last the apple drops out. So it is with a poor soul at the throne of grace. The Lord opens his hand and fills all living things with good. What opens his hand? The prayers of his children. They open one finger, then another, until at last the blessing falls.

Fifthly, if you pray importunately, you pray wakefully. He that prays must be deeply awake. His soul, heart, and understanding must be awake. A drowsy prayer is no powerful prayer. "Watch ye therefore, and pray always," (Luke 21:36). As a beggar, when he begs, is all awake—head, feet, hands—so must the soul be that means to succeed in prayer.

Sixthly, importunate prayer is assurance-getting prayer. It will not rest until it has assurance that God has heard. Wicked men presume that God hears them, but he does not. Even God's dear children may pray often and not be heard. "O Lord God of hosts, how long wilt thou be angry against the prayer of thy people?" (Psalm 80:4). If God is angry even with the prayers of his people, how then will he receive the prayers of those who live in sin? Their prayers vanish into the air like clouds.

"Behold, he prayeth," (Acts 9:11). What, did not Saul pray before? Yes, he had made many long prayers, or he could not have been a Pharisee. But now he truly prayed. Now his heart was lifted to God, as David's was: "Unto thee, O Lord, do I lift up my soul," (Psalm 25:1). Our hearts are like a bell lying on the ground—it makes no music until it is lifted up. Therefore, if you pray but do not lift up your heart to God, your prayer will be to your condemnation, as with the prayers of the wicked. But if you pray importunately, pray fervently, God will hear in mercy.

There are six or seven marks of a prayer that is not importunate; and he that prays in such a way may go to hell for all I know.

First, a *lazy* prayer. An importunate man works hard to bring up his petition; his understanding, his counsel, his skill, and his strength are all engaged. If the soul is importunate, then prayer is a labor. "Strive together with me in your prayers to God for me," (Romans 15:30). The word is labor with me in prayer. That man who plows his field and digs his vineyard prays for a good harvest by his labor. So it is with grace—if a man prays for repentance, faith, or any grace, yet will not use the means, he will never obtain it. God will not hear lazy beggars, those unwilling to follow their calling, who think they can get everything by begging alone. If they can have pardon of sin for begging, they will have it, but if they must labor in the means, they will not. Let such men know: God will not grant mercy to such lazy prayers. If you would have pardon of sin, you must labor for it, use the means, and watch over your own soul. God does not give grace by miracle, but by means.

Second, a prayer that is not full never prevails with God. An importunate prayer is a full prayer; it pours out the whole heart. "Trust in him at all times; ye people, pour out your heart before him," (Psalm 62:8). And again: "Pour out thine heart like water before the face of the Lord," (Lamentations 2:19). Some prayers are like tar poured from a tar-box—half sticks to the sides. So many pray half-heartedly. But God requires the whole heart. When you give thanks, do you labor to recall all his blessings? When you make petition, do you pour out all your heart before him, casting all your care upon God? If not, your prayer is *not* full.

Third, snatch-prayers are not importunate. When men pray by snatches, in fits, in fragments, because of sluggishness or because their minds are more eager on other business, such prayer is *worthless*. It is base devotion to gallop over your prayer only to be done quickly. "Ye said also, Behold, what a weariness is it! ... ye brought that which was torn, and the lame, and the sick; thus ye brought an offering: should I accept this of your hand? saith the Lord," (Malachi 1:13). So it is with ragged, snatched prayers. Many give God the rags of devotion—a piece in the morning, a piece at night—and think it will serve. But God asks, "Shall I accept this? What, a lame prayer?" No, he looks for a prayer that has its full strength and measure.

Fourth, silent prayers are not importunate. By silent prayer I do not mean when lips are still but the heart prays. I mean when men are silent in that which God expects them to insist upon. David made a prayer in Psalm 32, but he did not stand much on his adultery and murder. What does the text say? "When I kept silence, my bones waxed old through my roaring all the day long," (Psalm 32:3). Was he roaring and silent at once? Yes—he roared, but God counted it silence, because he did not confess the sin God required him to confess. Only when he said, "I acknowledged my sin unto thee, and mine iniquity have I not hid," then God forgave (Psalm 32:5). So with many: they cry to God for mercy, yet keep silence on the very sin they should confess. That man shall never be heard.

Have you been a drunkard? Do you think God will forgive because you mutter, "Lord, forgive me"? No, you must insist: "Against your Word I have been a drunkard. My conscience told me so, but I ignored it. Your Spirit stirred against me, and I resisted I have neglected many sermons. I have led others into drunkenness, and they may be in hell now because of me. If you cast me into hell, I am well repaid. I have returned to my sin like a dog to his vomit. For all my prayers you may damn me forever. Yet as I desire forgiveness, I covenant to leave this sin; if I return to it, I deserve damnation." Such prayer God loves.

Fifth, *faint* prayers are not importunate. Cold, lifeless prayers will never prevail with God. "The effectual fervent prayer of a righteous man availeth much," (James 5:16). Prayer must have heat in it, else it dies at God's altar. That man who prays faintly does not prize mercy, and so he prays as though he cared not whether he had it or not. But an importunate soul prays with zeal, his affections are set on fire. As Hannah prayed with such fervency that Eli thought she was drunk, so must our hearts boil over before God.

Sixth, *unbelieving* prayers are not importunate. "But let him ask in faith, nothing wavering," (James 1:6). He who prays without faith shall receive nothing. Many pray, but they doubt whether God hears them; they pray, but they stagger at the promise; they pray, but they question whether God will pardon them. Such prayers are not importunate. An importunate prayer comes with this confidence: "Lord, you have promised, and I will not let you go without the blessing. Though you kill me, yet will I trust in you. Though you delay, I will wait. Though you seem to frown, I will still plead your promise."

Seventh, *proud* prayers are not importunate. When men come in their own conceit, boasting of their righteousness, and standing on their own worth, their prayers are abomination. The Pharisee prayed, "God, I thank thee, that I am not as other men are," (Luke 18:11). He prayed proudly, and went away condemned. But the publican, smiting his breast, cried, "God be merciful to me a sinner," (v. 13). He prayed importunately, humbly, and was justified. God resists the proud, but gives grace to the humble. If your prayers are proud, you may roar to heaven, yet it will not profit.

These, then, are the marks of prayers that are not importunate: lazy prayers, half-hearted prayers, snatched prayers, silent prayers, faint prayers, unbelieving prayers, and proud prayers. He who prays in such a way may pray himself into hell. But he who prays with importunity, fervently, humbly, in faith, pouring out all his heart before God—he shall surely be heard at the throne of grace.

Fifthly, *seldom* prayer is no importunate prayer. When the soul contents itself with seldom coming before the throne of grace, it cannot be called importunate. An importunate soul is always frequenting the way of mercy and the gate of Christ; he is often at God's threshold, in all prayer and humility.

The most staggering drunkard in the world can sometimes restrain himself; the vilest adulterer in the world can sometimes abstain; even the devil is quiet so long as he is pleased. Likewise, the wicked may sometimes take a turn at prayer. But this is the difference: the importunate heart is consistent and frequent at the throne of grace. David prayed seven times a day (Psalm 119:164), and Hannah continued in prayer night and day (Luke 2:37).

Sixthly, *lukewarm* prayer is not importunate prayer. When a man prays without fervor, without laboring to wind up his soul to God in prayer, such prayer is useless. The one who prays outwardly only teaches God to deny his prayer. "And when ye spread forth your hands, I will hide mine eyes from you: yea, when ye make many prayers, I will not hear: your hands are full of blood," (Isaiah 1:15). *Qui frigide orat, docet negare*—*he who prays coldly teaches God to deny him.* They are like lukewarm water, never hot enough to boil away the blood. They may pray against their sins, but they never pray hotly enough to burn them away. If you would get pardon for all your sins—security, deadness of heart, and the rest—you must pray with a seething-hot heart. "Let them turn every one from his evil way ... and cry mightily unto God," (Jonah 3:8).

Seventhly and lastly, *wandering thoughts* in prayer keep prayer from being importunate. When a man prays and lets his heart go wool-gathering, he ruins his own devotion. I remember a story of an unworthy orator, who in an acclamation cried, "O earth! O heaven!" yet when he said "O heaven," he looked down to the earth, and when he said "O earth," he looked up to heaven. So it is with many: while they pray to God in heaven, their thoughts are fixed on the earth. Such prayers can never be importunate.

When a man prays, the Lord expects his heart to be fixed on his prayer. But our hearts leak, and even the best child of God will have distractions in prayer. These arise from four causes:

1. From corrupt nature. Even the holiest carry about a corrupt nature. They would perform duties better if they could, saying with Paul, "The good that I would I do not," (Romans 7:19).
2. From nature when curbed. The more grace restrains nature, the more restless it grows. A bird at liberty may sit still, but put it in a cage and it flutters, for its liberty is restrained. So, when grace curbs sin, the flesh grows skittish in duty. Therefore the apostle said, "I find then a law, that, when I would do good, evil is present with me," (Romans 7:21).
3. From Satan. As in Job, Satan stood at his right hand to resist him. Aegidius compared it to a plaintiff who puts in all manner of accusations to hinder the defendant. So, the devil casts in wandering thoughts to hinder the soul's suit before the throne of grace. But you must do as Abraham did when the birds came upon his sacrifice—he drove them away (Genesis 15:11). So must you drive away your wandering thoughts if you will gain fruit from your supplications.
4. From spiritual sluggishness. This creeps even upon the best if they are not watchful. For this

reason Paul cried out, "O wretched man that I am! who shall deliver me from the body of this death?" (Romans 7:24).

Now I do not speak of the children of God who are troubled with wandering thoughts in prayer. For the more distractions they have, the more earnest they are; they mourn like David, who said, "I mourn in my complaint, and make a noise," (Psalm 55:2). His prayer was vexed, and that made him mourn the more before God.

But for you who can let wandering thoughts stay with you and are not grieved by them—your prayers are not importunate. The heathen will rise in judgment against you and condemn you. I remember the story of a youth who, holding the golden censer with fire in it while standing in the temple with Alexander, had a coal fall upon his hand and burn his wrist. Yet, knowing what a sacred duty he was engaged in, he would not stir, but endured the pain until the service was done. This should shame those who let the least distraction draw away their hearts. Baal's priests will *condemn* you; they cut themselves with knives to stir themselves up to prayer. And shall we, who pray for our very souls, do it with loose and lazy hearts?

Think of it. Does a malefactor, when pleading for his life at the bar, let his mind wander to food, or to harlots, or to dogs? Was Jonah distracted with such thoughts in the belly of the whale? Was the thief on the cross, or Daniel in the lions' den, or the three children in the fiery furnace, or Paul in prison? No. They cried with all their hearts. And so must you, if your prayer is to be importunate.

Do you think that these prayed in such a way? What, shall I be at prayer and my mind in the fields? No, no; if I will pray, I must *melt* before God, bewail my sins, and be deeply affected in prayer. But, as long as I pray with a wandering heart, *I do not truly pray at all*. And as God said to Adam, "Where art thou?" (Genesis 3:9), so may he say to you: "Man, where are you? Are you at prayer, and yet your mind is at the mill? Is your mind on your oxen, while you are praying before me? What an indignity is this!" Should a man come to sue to the king and not pay attention to his own petition? Will not the king say, "Do you mock me? Do you know to whom you speak?" The Lord counts it a grievous sin when men come into his presence with such loose hearts.

Now, since these things are so, take this word of exhortation: *labor for importunate prayer*.

Prayer is the art of all arts; it enables a man for every other duty. It is the art of repentance, and of thanksgiving. Samuel confessed that if he did not have the art of prayer, he could not have the art of preaching. "Moreover as for me, God forbid that I should sin against the LORD in ceasing to pray for you: but I will teach you the good and the right way: Only fear the LORD, and serve him in truth with all your heart: for consider how great things he hath done for you," (1 Sam. 12:23-24). See the antithesis between these two words, "God forbid."

As if he had said, God forbid that I should cease to pray for you, for then I could not teach you the right way. A minister can never preach to his people if he does not pray for his people. Prayer is also the art of thanksgiving; a man cannot be thankful if he cannot pray. "What shall I render unto the LORD for all his benefits toward me? I will take the cup of salvation, and call upon the name of the LORD," (Psalm 116:12–13). That was the way David would be thankful. A servant is not a good servant unless he can pray for his master; see Abraham's servant in Genesis 24. Prayer helps a man perform every good duty. How do you think to profit by the Word unless you are fervent in prayer for God's blessing upon it? We can do nothing without begging.

Secondly, as prayer is the art of all arts, so it is the compendium of all divinity. To call zealously on the name of the Lord is to be a Christian. "For whosoever shall call upon the name of the Lord shall be saved," (Romans 10:13). Prayer includes repentance, humiliation, sorrow for sin, joy in God's goodness, thanksgiving for mercies, obedience to his commandments—yes, the whole duty of man. Therefore, we must labor to be importunate in prayer. Prayer is in itself *all good duties*. "The prayers of David the son of Jesse are ended," (Psalm 72:20). That is, all his repentance and every part of his humiliation and thanksgiving are summed up under the name of prayer. Therefore, make much of prayer; you cannot repent unless you first pray well.

Thirdly, prayer is a man's utmost refuge. He cannot have Christ except by prayer. It is bad enough for a man to be a drunkard, or to live in other sins; but if he yet has the spirit of prayer, there is still hope for him. But if a man sins and is not importunate in prayer, his condition is dreadful. "Have all the workers of iniquity no knowledge? ... they call not upon the LORD," (Psalm 14:4). Oh fearful condition!

Fourthly, prayer is what God's people always have, even if they have nothing else. It is the beggar's dish, so to speak. A beggar has no other way to live but by begging; therefore, he must beg earnestly. So it is with us—we have nothing to live on but prayer. All the promises of God are obtained by prayer. Suppose a man had nothing to live on but his fingers' ends—no house, no land, nothing to maintain wife and children but his daily labor. Would he not toil all day? That is how a Christian must treat prayer—it is his fingers' ends. When a house stands on one pillar, will not a man be most careful of that pillar? Prayer is our pillar; if it falls, all hope of salvation falls with it.

Fifthly, prayer has the *command* of mercy. We are such unprofitable servants that mercy will not deal with us unless commanded. Patience itself is reluctant to bear with us, we have provoked God so much. Unless mercy has a command from God, it will not receive any soul. When David begged for lovingkindness, he was importunate, or else mercy and lovingkindness would not have looked upon him (Psalm 42:8).

Sixthly, prayer is *God's delight*. "The sacrifice of the wicked is an abomination to the LORD: but the prayer of the upright is his delight," (Proverbs 15:8). Kings must be pleased, and so must the King of heaven. Nothing pleases him more than prayer.

Seventhly, importunate prayer is willing prayer. Many pray to God for mercy, and yet they are unwilling to have it, because they are not importunate. When a man's lust runs after the world and its pleasures, he cannot speed in prayer. But when the woman of Canaan was importunate, Christ said unto her, "O woman, great is thy faith: be it unto thee even as thou wilt," (Matthew 15:28). She had a will for grace.

Eighthly, importunate prayer is the only faithful prayer. A beggar never leaves a gentleman's door, as long as he believes he will get alms. So, as long as the soul is importunate with God, it shows that it believes. "O woman, great is thy faith," said Christ. Why? Because her importunity was great, therefore her faith was great.

The means to *gain* importunity in prayer are these:

First, labor to know your misery. "Praying always with all prayer and supplication in the Spirit ... and for me, that utterance may be given unto me," (Ephesians 6:18–19). They could not have prayed importunately unless they had known how Paul stood in need. So, unless you know your misery, you cannot be importunate. If a drunkard, whoremonger, Sabbath-breaker, or swearer knew that he must be damned, he would quickly seek deliverance.

Secondly, be sensible of your misery. Simon Magus knew his misery, but he was not sensible of it. He said, "Pray ye to the Lord for me," (Acts 8:24). If he had been sensible, he would have fallen down himself before the congregation and confessed his sin in a more heartfelt way.

Thirdly, observe the prayers of God's people, as the disciples did with Christ. Hearing Christ pray, they said, "Lord, teach us to pray," (Luke 11:1). They were so affected with his prayer that they longed for the same spirit. So, consider how God's people pray. They soar as if they would rend the heavens. If men would observe this, it would stir them.

Fourthly, get a stock of prayer. A man must be rich if he has stock in every market. So, if a man has a stock of prayer, he is sure to speed. "Ye also helping together by prayer for us," (2 Corinthians 1:11). If God lent his ear to the Corinthians when they prayed for Paul, then surely Paul's prayers were importunate.

Fifthly, labor to be full of good works. *Qui bene operatur, bene orat*—he who works well, prays well. Cornelius's alms and prayers came up together before God (Acts 10:4). If he had been guilty of drunkenness, that sin would have come up with his prayer. But because he was full of good works, his prayer was accepted. So, you cannot be importunate in prayer unless you are full of good works. Take heed that your sins do not cry louder in God's ears than your prayers.

Sixthly, reform your household. When Jacob was about to call on God, he said to his household, "Put away the strange gods that are among you," (Genesis 35:2).

Sermon 5:
The Necessity of Gospel-Obedience Part 1

Colossians 1:10, "That you might walk worthy of the Lord unto all pleasing, being fruitful unto every good work."

There is a double sense in these words:

First, in which we may not, nor cannot walk worthy of God.

Secondly, there is a sense wherein we may and must walk worthy of him.

The first sense, wherein we cannot walk worthy of God, is twofold.

First, we cannot walk worthy of God with an absolute worth of *exact* proportion; for in this sense even the angels of heaven *cannot* walk worthy of God. They bless God and praise him unceasingly, but God is *above* all blessing and praise (Nehemiah 9:5). Their holiness had a beginning, but God is infinite. Oh then, how much less can we walk worthy of God!

Secondly, we cannot walk worthy of God with a sinless worth of a mortified condignity, so worthily as we might have done if we had not had sin; for we are compassed with the flesh and sin, which leads us into all impieties. In this respect John said, "I am not worthy," (Luke 3:16). It was no idle complement in that good man, that he was not worthy to untie Christ's shoe-latchet, or to carry his books after him, as we use to speak. It is certain, in regard of sin which makes us unfit to do any duty to God, that God is worthy of better service than the best of us can perform, and of better attendance than we can give him.

Nevertheless, there is a sense wherein we may and must walk worthy of God. This also is twofold:

First, *quoad dignitatem non repugnantiae* (as to the dignity of non-repugnancy). As a miserly or sparing servant is unworthy of a bountiful master, or a drunkard of a godly master, there is a repugnancy between a master and such a servant. "He that taketh not his cross, and followeth after me, is not worthy of me," (Matthew 10:38). In this sense we must walk worthy of God—that is, not contrary to God.

Secondly, this worthy includes *dignitatem condecentiae* (a dignity of suitability). Walk *worthy* of God—that is, suitably to him. There must be a correspondence between Christ and those that are his, between the children of God and God himself. We must walk answerable to him. God is holy, gracious, merciful, and so must we walk suitably to those attributes; not to deal basely with God, who has dealt bountifully with us, who has delivered us from hell and helps us to heaven. Let us not then put unworthy tricks upon God, but let us walk as men renewed. So much for the sense.

This speech is directed to the professors of the gospel of Christ in Colossae. For first, Epaphras had reported that there were godly souls in that city.

Secondly, as it was reported, so this report came to Paul. "We heard of your faith in Christ Jesus," (Colossians 1:4). I, Paul, heard so; and therefore Paul directs his speech. As if he should say (for so it is in the ninth verse): I hear that there are professors among you; now I pray God that you walk worthy of God. You profess Christ and his Word; I pray to God you may walk worthy of the master you serve.

Observe here: those that profess Christ must walk worthy of Christ; worthy of Christ whom they *say* they serve.

This is further commanded, and that expressly, in 1 Thessalonians 2:12: "That ye would walk worthy of God." Think not that this is a duty left to your choice. No, no, says the Apostle: you know how we have exhorted and charged you. As if he should say: I have given many exhortations to this purpose; I have begged that you would do so (verse 11). I have encouraged and comforted those that have done so; I commanded the unwilling; and you know it. I tell you this is a duty of great consequence.

First, because he has called you to be Christians. Now it is a shame for you to be unworthy of the calling whereunto you are called. It is fitting, if a man be called unto a calling, that he be worthy of it. When a wicked and unjust man is preferred to be a judge, God knows he is a very unworthy man for that calling. A *licentious* divine in a pulpit is unworthy of that vocation. It is a shame that a man should be unworthy of the calling whereunto he is called. We are called to be Christians; is it not a shame that a man should be unworthy of the vocation the Lord has called him unto? "I therefore, the prisoner of the Lord, beseech you that ye walk worthy of the vocation wherewith ye are called," (Ephesians 4:1). You are called to be Christians by Christ: I beseech you consider this, and be worthy of this calling. Are you Christians, and yet careless and secure? Will you not walk as Christ walked? Shall a man be a Christian, and carry himself dishonestly, contrary to the gospel? What a shame is this!

Secondly, the gospel of God by which we are called is a blessed calling. The Lord Jesus tells us what the gospel is in Luke 4:18: it is riches to the poor, sight to the blind, deliverance to captives, a gospel of peace and liberty. It has many excellent names in Scripture. Now this is the gospel by which you are called from being damned wretches to be the sons of God. That man is unworthy of freedom who is content to be a slave. He is unworthy of the blessed things the gospel brings who still walks in sin. What, will you still be captives to hell? Will you go on in your old ways still? Will you live after the imaginations of your own hearts still, even though you are called by the gospel? Have you the gospel of a kingdom, and will you not obey it when it calls you to be kings? What an unworthy thing is this, that a man should not behave himself worthy of the gospel by which he is called! "Only let your conversation be as it becometh the gospel of Christ," (Philippians 1:27). For men to be covetous, proud, drunkards, and so on still, when we have the gospel to draw us out of these sins—surely it is a shame, and we are unworthy of this gospel.

Thirdly, because we are called to repentance. As we are called by the gospel, so by the gospel we are called to repentance; therefore, we must walk worthy. Is it repentance enough to hear a sermon, or do any good duty? No, no; these are not fruits worthy the name of repentance (Luke 3:8). I do not mean worthy to be repented of, but not worthy of the *name* of repentance. For a man to put his finger in his eye and cry, "Lord"—is this worthy the name of repentance? No, no; it must be a deeper mourning than this. True, many repent, but they do not repent *enough*; they must bring forth fruits *worthy* of repentance.

Fourthly, because if we do not walk worthy of God, the wisdom of God will not count us for his servants. A master, if he is wise, will not keep a servant that will not do his business. If the master has cattle to be looked after, and other work abroad to be done, if his servant lies and sleeps all day, or sits in the alehouse and neglects his master's business—surely, if the master is but worldly-wise, he will not keep such a servant. In 1 Samuel 30:13, an Amalekite turned away his servant because he was sick. This was hard dealing.

Nevertheless, that man that will not walk worthy, that will not look to the charge God has given him, is unworthy to be God's servant. The Lord has abundance of business to be done: commandments to be kept, sacraments to be received, much employment to be carried out. Shall he hire servants and yet do the work himself? Will any man keep a dog, and bark himself? That man is not worthy of God who will not do his business. Therefore, the wisdom of God will turn us out of doors, because we leave his work and fall to wrangling among ourselves. What division is there among us? What heart-burning between neighbors? What coldness in religion? And yet God has haste of business to be dispatched. Why are not his commandments regarded, his promises desired, his judgments feared? Certainly, the Lord expects that we should go about these things, and we are unworthy if we do not.

Fifthly, if we will not walk worthy of God, then it is for his glory to leave his sanctuary. It is not for a master's credit to keep a servant that will discredit him. To keep a whoremonger, or a base companion—what will honest men think? They will say, "Is not he naught himself that keeps such ragged company about him?" All the dishonor lies on the master. So, it is not for the honor of God to suffer such to be within the company of professors of his name, who dishonor his name and cause the gospel to be blasphemed by those that are without. As soon as Elisha's servant Gehazi had abused him, he sent him packing: "He went out from his presence a leper as white as snow," (2 Kings 5:27). He stayed no longer with him. Why? Because he had dishonored him. And what might Naaman think? "Will he now take something? Even now he would take nothing—has he so quickly repented of his kindness?" Though Naaman did not argue so, yet he might have, and for all we know, such thoughts entered his mind. But however, Gehazi greatly dishonored his master, and therefore his master sent him away. Even so, if we do not walk worthy of God, he will turn us out of doors.

You that are the servants of God, and are found with a lie, undermining one another, or living uncharitably with each other—this is a dishonor to God. This is not to walk worthy of God; it disgraces the gospel and casts aspersions on it. Therefore, as it concerns the glory of God, so we ought to walk worthy of God. What will the world think if professors walk loosely and are caught tripping? What will the world say? "God keep me from being a Puritan; I would rather be a Papist." And in this way the name of Christ comes to be blasphemed for your sakes. These men say, "Come, come, I warrant you, for all this, he will lie if need be, though he says, Yes, verily." In this way religion and the gospel of Christ are brought into question by the world, because of you who do not walk worthy of God. Indeed, by reason of this, God cannot hire servants to do his work. Beloved, God has sent us out to hire servants; many would willingly come in, but because they see and think that those who profess the name of Christ are dissemblers, Puritans, and hypocrites, they refuse. And so they say, as once the Indians said of the Spaniards, "If these men are the servants of Christ, I will never be his servant." So also they say, "If these men are the servants of God, Lord keep me from them." What a cursed thing this is!

Sixthly, if we do not walk worthy of God, we put great indignity upon him. A worthy man cannot endure to deal with unworthy things; and shall a Christian serve God in an unworthy way? No master, whether in heaven, on earth, or in hell, will have a servant unworthy of him. This is why men swear, lie, and live like devils incarnate—because the devil will have them *worthy of hell*. The world lets men cheat and dissemble, because the world will have them worthy of the world. All masters, whether the world, the flesh, or the devil, expect their servants to be worthy of them. And do you then think that the Lord will not require his servants to walk worthy of him? "Be not deceived; God is not mocked," (Galatians 6:7). Do you come into his house, hear his Word, and yet will not obey it? Do you come to a sacrament, and yet keep drinking, gaming, and dicing at home? Do you go under the name of a Christian, and yet live in your sins, clinging to some secret lust, whether it be swearing, lying, or adultery? Take heed, I say—God will not be mocked. For men to go under the name of God's children, and yet not serve and obey him, is to make a mockery of God. But God will not be mocked.

"Oh," says one, "my father will never like it if I am so strict and precise; and as for my mother, she cannot abide a Puritan." Another says, "I cannot keep my children unless I put my money to interest," and the like.

But what says Christ? "He that loveth father or mother more than me is not worthy of me," (Matthew 10:37). Do you argue this way, and yet hope to be a Christian? Do you plead self-interest, and yet hope to be accounted a Christian? What a mockery is this! Even nature abhors it.

I remember the story of a boy who, being at Lyons, saw two men: one was tall but had a short cloak, and the other was short but had a long cloak. The boy thought it unseemly, so he took the long cloak and put it on the tall man's back, and the short cloak on the short man's back—and then it pleased him. So also, is it seemly that any of us should wear the long robes of Christianity, and yet be short in obedience? That we should go under the name of the people of God, and yet not behave ourselves suitably?

In this place there is no room for Papists to establish merit for themselves; the Apostle intends no such matter here. For we are not our own, and therefore cannot merit. We are taught to pray, "Give us this day our daily bread," (Matthew 6:11). We have not one morsel of bread unless we beg it. And when we have done all we can (and who does so?), yet we are but unprofitable servants. But suppose we could merit all righteousness—yet all our ability is from God. Again, suppose we are righteous—what is that to him? If we are holy—what is that to him? If we are damned, he is never the worse; if we are saved, he is not the better. If we keep all his commandments, it is still his mercy that saves us.

He shows mercy to thousands. To whom? "To them that love me, and keep my commandments," (Exodus 20:6). To one that keeps God's commandments, it is his love to save him, it is his love that has mercy on him.

The Church of Rome talks much of their well-doing; but in the meantime, what becomes of their sins? They ought to go and suffer for their sins, and then come and talk of merit. Do they talk of merit before they have satisfied for their sins? The law must first be satisfied. And when they have endured hellfire, world without end, then let them talk of merit. The Lord does not mean that we must walk worthy so as to merit anything. For suppose all the sufferings of this life, and all the torments of the world that all the saints of God have endured, were laid upon one man, and he bore them all—yet they are not worthy of the glory that shall be revealed (Romans 8:18). Here, then, is no room for Papists' merits. Yet we must walk worthy of God with suitability. And if we do not, the Lord will not own us. You know the story of the guests in the gospel and how they were invited to the supper. One pretended one excuse, another a different excuse. One had married a wife and said he could not come—yet surely he might have brought her with him. Another had bought oxen, and so forth. But what follows in the text? "They which were bidden were not worthy," (Matthew 22:8). Therefore, they shall not taste of my supper. So, some excuse themselves for their sins, saying it is their nature, or that one occasion or another hinders them. None who are unworthy of God shall taste of the mercy of God, neither in the pardon of their sins nor in salvation. No, you will not get even so much as a taste of Christ if you do not walk worthy of the gospel of Christ.

The truth of this will appear in the use, if we consider what this worthy walking is.

First, we must be, as it were, the very nature of God. As Peter speaks, we must show forth the virtues of him that has called us, that we may declare what a glorious God, what a blessed Redeemer, and righteous Judge we have, and admire his goodness in calling us out of darkness into his marvelous light. We must be holy as he is holy (1 Peter 1:15). How does it suit with the nature of God, when we do not walk worthy of him? God is just (2 Corinthians 1:3). How unworthy, then, are we when we are cruel, unmerciful, and unjust? God is a God of peace (1 Corinthians 14:33). How unworthy, then, are we when we live in strife and bitterness with one another? We are the image of God if we please him (1 Corinthians 11:7). What a shame, dishonor, and wrong it is to God that we should bear his image, and yet be nothing like him! Should a glorious king see a deformed picture of himself, surely he would punish the one who painted him so. And shall we go as the image of God, the God of all glory, and yet be vile, unclean, negligent, and careless, and still claim to be his image? What do we make of God? Will he not be angry, and will not his wrath burn like fire? What—am I a drunkard, a whoremaster, and so forth—is this my picture? Surely God cannot endure this.

Secondly, consider the relation we have to God. We are the children of God; we are begotten of the Father. Does God *beget* monsters? Does God beget such children? We profess ourselves servants of God; the ground of that relation is that we are at God's command. Did God command us to carry out the duties of religion in such a way?

No, no, beloved; if we are servants, we must be at his command. We profess ourselves sheep of his pasture; but do we live as if we fed on his commandments? Is this to live worthy of the provision Christ has given us, which is the rich food of salvation? How unworthy is this? "If then I be a father, where is mine honour? and if I be a master, where is my fear?" (Malachi 1:6). Is it not rather to dishonor God, that a child should have a worthy man for his father, and yet be a lout himself? What indignity is this that we put on God? Let us examine ourselves whether we walk *worthy* of God or *not*. I speak to the professors of the gospel; for it is certain that those who do not profess it are unworthy. You that are still in the gall of bitterness and in the bond of iniquity are not worthy.

For first, Christianity is a trade. Whatever profession you are of, that is your trade. Will a man say to a physician, "What, can you not keep your medicine to yourself? Must you make profession of it?" Or will a man say to a shoemaker, "Can you not keep your shoes and your trade to yourself?" So, Christianity is a profession, and you are unworthy of it unless you profess it.

Secondly, what is the purpose of a trade? It will do a man no good unless he profess it. Every man in his calling lives by his calling; then, if he lives by it, he must walk worthy of it. A lawyer may die despite his calling, if he does not profess it. Do you walk in no calling nor profession? Surely, you will get no living by it.

Thirdly, Christianity is an *order*. If a man is a Papist, yet he cannot be a Franciscan unless he profess himself of that order. So, if we are Christians, Christ is the Father of that order. "Consider the Apostle and High Priest of our profession, Christ Jesus," (Hebrews 3:1). He is the Father of all Christianity, and you cannot be a Christian unless you profess that order. "Let your light so shine before men, that they may see your good works, and glorify your Father which is in heaven," (Matthew 5:16). Otherwise, you do not walk worthy of God. I speak this to those who profess Christ; for a man may profess a trade, and yet not walk worthy of it.

First, if we walk worthy of God, then our labors must answer all the cost God has expended on us. That ground is unworthy of tillage which does not repay the cost bestowed on it. That scholar is unworthy to be maintained who does not answer the cost of his parents. So, my beloved, if you walk worthy of God, you will answer the charges that God has laid out on you. It has cost God his Son to redeem you—and what are you the better? The work of his Spirit comes to enlighten us, the labor of his ministers to teach us—and what are we the better for all this? It has cost God abundance of mercy to allure us, abundance of judgment to terrify us, many corrections, and above all, he has been patient to bear with us—and this is mercy of mercies. A man will show all he has before he shows his patience; he may show himself kind, but if he is much wronged, he will say, "What, will you try my patience?" I tell you, God has allowed his patience to be *wearied* by us for a long time, and he has been at great cost with us. But have we answered it? If we have not, we are unworthy of God.

God has been at great cost to make you love one another—and shall there be heart-burning still? Good ground brings forth herbs fit for use, not just herbs, but herbs fit for use. So, if you are God's children, you will bring forth fruit fit for God. Otherwise, if God has spent all this cost and you remain secure, strangers still to one another, and never the better, then you are near to cursing. Your labor is unprofitable in the Word, and you do not answer the cost God has expended on you. I fear God will remove his candlestick, or, if he continue it, you will have hardness of heart with it. For since these divisions have arisen, how has the number of believers decreased? When was one converted? When was a whoremaster or a drunkard renewed—unless it was only to take a higher degree in sin? No, no, the gospel has ceased to bring forth children; and surely this is the cause: we do not walk worthy of it.

Secondly, if we walk worthy of God, then we walk with God in white. "Thou hast a few names even in Sardis which have not defiled their garments; and they shall walk with me in white: for they are worthy," (Revelation 3:4). In white, that is, in true love and holiness, with white robes of purity, clothed in the righteousness of Christ. But if you are of the black qualities of the world, you do not walk worthy; you do not edify yourselves nor others. This kind of walking belongs to the men of the world—it is for them to stand still in religion, to hear and not to practice. These are black qualities. But if you walk aright, you walk with me in white, says God. Those who walk aloof walk unworthily, like base rogues who are not admitted into the king's presence.

Thirdly, if we walk worthy of God, we do not disappoint God's account. God accounts us sincere and undefiled, as a virgin unspotted, pure in heart. Such as are renewed, the Lord calls all his children by this name. Now if you walk so that the world may accuse you of pride, covetousness, hatred, or any other vice, this is not to walk worthy of God, but to disparage God's account. God counts you righteous, and the world censures you and says you are not, and that because of your bad behavior. So, God's judgment seems not to be right. "They which shall be accounted worthy to obtain that world, and the resurrection from the dead, neither marry, nor are given in marriag" (Luke 20:35). They that enjoy God's glory are counted worthy—God counts them worthy, Christ counts them worthy, conscience and the world count them worthy. But do you think the wicked will say at the last day that they were worthy? No, no; this would be a disparagement to God.

Fourthly, if we walk worthy of God, then we are importunate beggars. That beggar who will not beg hard is unworthy of alms; so we are unworthy of mercy if we do not beg hard for it. "Watch ye therefore, and pray always, that ye may be accounted worthy," (Luke 21:36).

Fifthly, if we walk worthy of God, then we *add* humiliation to every duty we do to God. It is true, all our prayers are not accepted unless they are worthy. Our receiving the sacrament is cursed in God's sight unless it is done worthily. Yet not as though there were any inherent righteousness in man. No, no. "Lord, trouble not thyself: for I am not worthy that thou shouldest enter under my roof," (Luke 7:6). That is, I do not count myself worthy. Here is the worthiness of all our works, if we pray in faith, and add humility to our prayers. We must obey God and add humility to that obedience. We must add humiliation to every good duty. So that if we are worthy, we are the more humbled. This duty is of great moment. It is such a duty that if we walk not worthy of God in humiliation, we are not capable of the gospel, nor of the pardon of sin, if we are not content to be ruled by Christ. "And into whatsoever city or town ye shall enter, enquire who in it is worthy; and there abide till ye go thence. And when ye come into an house, salute it. And if the house be worthy, let your peace come upon it: but if it be not worthy, let your peace return to you," (Matthew 10:11, 12, 13). The peace of God's ministers is peace to the conscience; and the conscience is at peace if sin is pardoned. So then, if this place, this congregation, is not worthy that they should have the pardon of sin preached, they are not capable of it. The world must be pulled down, self-will and self-lust must be subdued and mortified, to do as the Lord wills. That man is not capable of the gospel who will not be ruled by it.

In the second place, let us consider: if we walk not worthy of God, we walk worthy of something else. If not of God, then of hell, vengeance, and condemnation. Let us assure ourselves, of whatever we are worthy, that we shall have. I do not speak of worthiness of *proportion*. Let a man be ignorant, if he is judged worthy of hell, then to hell he shall go. None shall go to hell but those who are unworthy of heaven; and none shall go to heaven but those who have the *tokens* of heaven about them. "For they have shed the blood of saints and prophets, and thou hast given them blood to drink; for they are worthy," (Revelation 16:6). As she was worthy of blood, so God gave her blood to drink her fill. So, when men walk on in their sinful courses, as they are worthy, so shall they have.

Secondly, you are guilty of Christ if you do not walk worthy of Christ. It is a damnable thing for a man to be thought or found guilty of perjury; but to be thought or found guilty of Christ—this is the greatest of all. Beloved, you are guilty of Christ if you do not walk worthy of Christ. See it in one branch of a Christian's walk: if a man receives the sacrament unworthily, he is guilty of Christ (1 Corinthians 11:27). If a man walks unworthily in any *one* duty, he is guilty of Christ, and the death of Christ shall be laid upon him. Oh, what then will become of those who walk unworthily in all the duties of Christianity? Judas betrayed Christ, and you are guilty; Pilate condemned him, and you are guilty; so also with the rest. His blood lies on your soul, and you shall answer for it if you do not get an interest into Christ. In this way you see, if we walk unworthily in one duty, we are guilty of all.

Thirdly, if you do not walk worthy of Christ, you shall be condemned. The sentence of condemnation is upon you forever. "For he that eateth and drinketh unworthily, eateth and drinketh damnation to himself," (1 Corinthians 11:29). And this is but one branch. So he that prays, or professes the name of Christ unworthily—whatever the duty is—if he does not labor to do it suitably to God, it is his damnation. That prisoner is unworthy of a pardon who will not stand to the conditions of his pardon and be ruled by the judge. Even so, you who will not walk holily according to the conditions of the gospel are not worthy of pardon, and you shall never enjoy it. For the Lord knows beforehand who are worthy walkers before him. Has God children here, and would they be so accounted? Let them walk worthy of God; let their light shine; let them labor to repay the cost that God has laid out; walk with Christ in all your ways, for this is to walk worthy of God in all pleasing. Let this suffice for exhortation.

Sermon 6:
The Necessity of Gospel Obedience Part 2

Colossians 1:10, "That ye might walk worthy of the Lord unto all pleasing, being fruitful in every good work."

The Apostle, having already set before us the various duties of walking worthy of God, concerning which we have spoken, now comes to enlarge upon them. He does this in two ways: first, generally, *unto all pleasing*; and secondly, particularly, in the various duties in which we are to please God—namely, to walk worthy, to be fruitful in every good work, and to increase in the knowledge of God *unto all pleasing* (as it is in the original).

Some would interpret *all pleasing* as "pleasing all men"; but this would be *sinful*. For if a man will be a man-pleaser, he cannot please God. What then? Does the Apostle exhort us to sin? God forbid. Would he have us strive to please all men? That would be flattery. No, there is no such thing in the original. It is not the adjective "in all pleasing," that is, pleasing to all; but the substantive, "unto all-pleasing," that is, *to all manner of pleasing*. Labor to walk according to the gospel, being guided in all your ways by its light, so that you may please God in all things. This is what it means to walk worthy of the Lord—namely, in all manner of pleasing to him.

And this is not impossible.

First, because God is not a rigorous God, but kind, loving, and gracious, full of compassion and kindness—a God *easy to please*. Really? There are some men who can never be pleased; they are so captious, so full of exceptions and humors, that no man can make them content. But God is a kind God, abundant in goodness and truth; therefore, *it is possible* for a man to please God. It is true, if God required obedience in strict rigor, holiness in strict rigor, then indeed it would be impossible to please him, for he would need servants of another sort than we are. But the Lord deals kindly; he demands obedience from us *according to the gospel*. "When a man's ways please the Lord," says the wise man (Proverbs 16:7). Here we may note that it is possible for a man to walk so that his ways may please God.

Secondly, as God is not rigorous, so there is a way in which we may walk to please him, and that is the way of sincerity. It was God's charge to Abraham (Genesis 17:1). We must be faithful in our callings. See it also in David: "I will praise the name of God with a song, and will magnify him with thanksgiving. This also shall please the Lord better than an ox or bullock that hath horns and hoofs," (Psalm 69:30–31). To be thankful and obedient to his commandments is the way to please God.

Thirdly, the Lord has shown us this way. He might have left it to us to discover, or he might have sent us to hell for our ignorance. He might have left us to study out what would please him, or, like a harsh master, refused to *tell us* what he desired. But here appears the love of God: as there is a way, so he has revealed this way to us. "This is my beloved Son, in whom I am well pleased; hear ye him," (Matthew 17:5). As if he had said, Go to my Son; he will teach you what pleases me, for in him I am well pleased. Not merely *with him*, though that is true, but *in him*. Get to him, be governed by him, be grafted into him—this is the way to please me. This is my *Beloved*.

Lastly, as God has shown us this way, so there are those who have walked in it before us. The children of God, in all ages, have labored to please him, as a child labors to please his father (Hebrews 11:5).

In this way you see it is possible to please God.

Secondly, as it is possible, so it is also a most fitting duty. It is most proper and suitable that we should labor to please God.

For first, God is a *great* king. Now great men, as you know, expect to be pleased. A man cannot speak to a king without saying, "If it please the king." "If it please the king," said Esther (Esther 1:19). Such a style belongs to greatness; it is fit that greatness should be accompanied with honor. Now who is so great as God? Therefore, it is fitting that his servants should please him.

Secondly, as God is great, so his pleasure is a good pleasure. Therefore, it is fitting he should be pleased. It is called here "the good pleasure of his will"

(Ephesians 1:5). Whatever God's pleasure is, it is always good; therefore, it is fitting he be pleased, because his pleasure is always reasonable. It is not always fitting to please men, for their desires are often wicked. See it in Ahasuerus: his pleasure was once to extirpate the Jews. Darius's pleasure was to seal an idolatrous decree. Pharaoh's pleasure was to lay heavy burdens on God's people. Herod's pleasure was to put James to death, and this pleased the Jews also. You see, then, their pleasures were wicked. Men's pleasures are not always good, and therefore not always fit to please. But God is always good, and therefore it is right and equitable always to please him.

Fourthly, if we will not, our betters will; and therefore, it is fitting that we should. Christ, who is far better than we, always did what pleased God (John 8:29). The angels of heaven also think it fitting—they bless the Lord, and they too are better than we (Psalm 103:21). If they think it right to please God, how much more should we? We reason with our children this way: "Will you not do as I tell you? Your betters do so." So it is with us—our *betters* please God, and so should we.

Fifthly, it is most suitable to our consciences that we should do so. For if we do not please God, our consciences will accuse us. "Beloved, if our heart condemn us not, then have we confidence toward God. And whatsoever we ask, we receive of him, because we keep his commandments, and do those things that are pleasing in his sight," (1 John 3:21–22). The pleasing of

God is set forth as that which pleases our consciences. And can there be a more fitting duty than that which, if neglected, will make our own consciences charge us with rebellion? Such is the duty of pleasing God. It is natural in the conscience of all men that God must be pleased. How often do we read in heathen books, "If it please God"? It is also a common phrase in the mouths of many. Therefore, it is a most fitting duty.

Sixthly, it is a duty most suitable to human society. If all men would labor to please God, there would be no hatred, no slander, no quarrels. Oh, what a blessed life might we live if we all labored to please God! This is the true ground of all good fellowship. But what was the reason the Jews were contrary to all men? It was this: because they did not please God (1 Thessalonians 2:15). When every man pleases himself in his own lusts and desires, then there must be contrariety among men. For one man's will is contrary to another's—one will have this, another will have that. But if all would submit their wills to God's will, and agree in him, there would be no contrariety among men.

Thirdly, as it is a possible and a fitting duty, so it is also a large duty; it extends, as the expositors observe, to all our thoughts, words, and deeds. It must be carried out at all times, in all places, and in all respects. It is, I say, a large duty, and I will show it in six things.

First, it is the end of all our duties. What duty is there for a Christian to undertake except that he is to please God in it? Why do we hear, pray, receive the sacrament, believe, repent, or suffer injuries for Christ's sake, but that we may please God? Why must children obey their parents, except that in doing so they may please God? I can go about no duty, but if I mean to do it rightly, I must set this as my end—that I may please God.

Secondly, it is large in that it is the most acceptable of all duties, and indeed the very form and life of all performances. Prayer is an abomination to God unless we please him in that action. The pleasing of God is that which puts life into the duty we undertake. "But my God shall supply all your need according to his riches in glory by Christ Jesus. Now unto God and our Father be glory for ever and ever. Amen," (Philippians 4:19–20). The Apostle here joins together the acceptable and the well-pleasing; and they cannot be separated. If any sacrifice is well-pleasing, it must needs be acceptable to God. Therefore, it is pleasing, because it makes every duty acceptable.

Thirdly, it is large in that it cannot be confined to any place or time. We must not only be godly at church, but at home also; not only behave well in the company of the godly, but we must be holy in all companies and please God everywhere. We must labor to please him wherever we are. It is not a duty restricted to any single place. Shall a man please God at a sermon, and then displease him abroad by drunkenness or whoredom? Shall we think to please God in such a place where for shame we dare not break out into unsavory speech, but at another place give full vent to every ungodliness? This is not pleasing God, but the very contrary. No, it is not limited to time or place. We must please God not only during prayer, but after prayer; not only during the sermon, but when the sermon is ended. Therefore, labor to please God at all times—not on Sundays only, but on weekdays also. Many will read on the Sabbath, but never else. But this is a duty to be performed always. It is not like hearing, which cannot be performed continually. No, it is a general duty. It is, as Aristotle would say, a universal. "I will walk before the Lord in the land of the living," (Psalm 116:9). *Placebo Domino*—I will please the Lord. This contains the sum of all religion.

[Objection.] But the largeness of this duty appears in that it extends to all things. Is it not larger than the duty of servants to please their masters? Yet servants must labor to please their masters in all things (Titus 2:9). How then can the duty of pleasing God be larger?

[Answer.] True it is, servants must please their masters in all things—that is, in all things commanded of God. Otherwise they may not. For when the thing is forbidden by God, it is nothing but a privation. Sin is a privation. An idol is nothing. All sins are as idols—they are nothing but the lack of God's image where it should be, and the lack of conformity to his Word. So, the duty of pleasing man is bounded within another duty; but the duty of pleasing God is without limitation.

Fifthly, it is large in that it is an everlasting duty. It will remain when other duties cease. Prayer, faith, repentance, weeping, mourning—these shall cease when God's children come to heaven. They will pray no more, fast no more. These duties shall end. But this duty—pleasing God—remains forever. It is a duty we must carry to our graves, yes, into another world. It is the fruit of all other duties. We are trained by prayer, by hearing, and by all other exercises, as by an apprenticeship, that we might learn this one art of well-pleasing God. If we have not learned this art, we are not capable of entering into life. So that, in some sense, it is above the commandments. We keep the commandments that we may please God. This is the crown and end of all our obedience. Not as though it could be more than the commandments, but rather that the pleasing of God is the very sum and upshot of our obedience to him.

Sixthly, it is large in that it is the whole duty of the new man. Only those who are new creatures in Christ can please God. The unregenerate cannot please him. Let them give alms, let them do outwardly good actions, yet if they are not new creatures, they cannot please God. Though their deeds may seem good in form or in meaning, yet they are worthless in the hands of an unregenerate man. "So then they that are in the flesh cannot please God," (Romans 8:8). He does not speak here of those who are married—for Zacharias and Elizabeth were married, and they pleased God—but of

Sermon 6: Gospel Obedience Part 1

those who walk after the flesh, unregenerate, unsanctified, unpurified, living in sin. Such as these can never please God. In this way you see it is the whole duty of *the new man*.

Fourthly, as it is possible, fitting, and large, so it is also a necessary duty. The Apostle sets a "must" and an "ought" upon it: "For ye know what commandments we gave you by the Lord Jesus. For this is the will of God, even your sanctification," (1 Thessalonians 4:2–3). It must be done; there is a necessity laid upon it.

First, we have no saving grace unless we labor to please God. It comes from God's good pleasure, and it returns to God's good pleasure. God is well pleased in his image, and grace is the image of God. Therefore, if a man does not please God, it is because he has no grace. You think Christ died for you? You believe a lie if you have no saving grace. "Wherefore we receiving a kingdom which cannot be moved, let us have grace, whereby we may serve God acceptably with reverence and godly fear," (Hebrews 12:28). As if the Apostle would say, without grace it is impossible to please him. Therefore, you see it is very necessary to please God. It is as necessary as grace, and without it we are damned.

Secondly, if we do not please God, what a wretched case we are in! If God is not pleased to spare us, we cannot be saved. Now a man will be sure to please the one who can hang him; he will not willingly stir up his displeasure. In Acts 12, when Herod was displeased, they labored to turn away his wrath and made friends.

So, we depend on God—our souls, bodies, and eternal happiness or destruction all lie in his hand. And if he is not pleased, what benefit can we expect? Would you have mercy, and yet not please God? You deceive yourself. Because Esther pleased the king, he showed her kindness (Esther 2:17). And God will never show us kindness unless we *please* him. No man is so foolish as to heap good turns upon one who will not please him. How then can we have the good pleasure of God when we will not *seek* to please him? "By faith Enoch was translated that he should not see death; and was not found, because God had translated him: for before his translation he had this testimony, that he *pleased* God" (Hebrews 11:5). God would never have brought him to heaven if he had not been pleased with him. So, before he translates you from earth to heaven, before he delivers you from damnation, you must be sure to please God.

Thirdly, if we do not labor to please God, we are always in infinite danger. In the morning he may strike us down, or we may perish in our sleep, or in any action we undertake. Who knows what mischief may befall us if we do not please God? If a man is found a traitor to the king, we know what the king will do to him. "The king's wrath is as the roaring of a lion," (Proverbs 19:12). Oh then, what is the displeasure of the Judge of the living and the dead? If God is displeased with us, what shall become of us? We cannot eat a meal in safety; we may be choked at the table for all we know. We cannot be secure for one moment. It may be this very moment he intends to disgrace you, to lay rottenness on your heart. It may be, he will strike you with the curse of heaven before you return home, and you shall be seen no more. But if you please God—"Go thy way, eat thy bread with joy, and drink thy wine with a merry heart; for God now accepteth thy works", (Ecclesiastes 9:7)—come what may, nothing can come amiss to those who please the Lord. But if your ways do not please the Lord, you live in a damnable condition.

If it is so that the duty of pleasing God is possible, fitting, large, and necessary, then three sorts of men are condemned.

First, those that do not please God. Do you think it pleases God that there should be so many alehouses in a town where the gospel has been so long taught? Do you think it pleases God that there should be so many *profane Esaus*, who walk after the stubbornness of their own hearts? Do you think it pleases God that you despise those who think best of his Word? Do you think it pleases God that your families remain in disorder, that after so much preaching many of you *still* live in your sins? Is this pleasing to God? Consider what you bring upon yourselves—wrath, even wrath to the uttermost. It is a dreadful thing for a man to bring the wrath of a king upon himself: "You shall not do this, on pain of our displeasure." And dare you do it? If the wrath of a king is so great and fearful, what then is the wrath of the eternal God, to the uttermost? It is destruction and damnation to the uttermost. God will show no mercy to those who make no conscience of pleasing him.

Secondly, this condemns those who please men. If it is so necessary to please God, what will become of those who make it their work to please men? And there are many such, who carry tales and run about with slanders—why? Because they would please this man or that man. Such are many of your children and servants who spend their time in alehouses, drawing pot after pot, because it pleases their master that it should be so. But what will become of this in the end? "For do I now persuade men, or God? or do I seek to please men? for if I yet pleased men, I should not be the servant of Christ", (Galatians 1:10). *If* I am not the servant of God or of Christ, then I must be the servant of the devil. Even I Paul, if I sought to please men, I would not be a servant of Jesus Christ.

Thirdly, this condemns those who please themselves. There are many who are self-pleasers, walking after their own wills, self-conceits, self-desires, and self-affections. It pleases them to drink, to swagger, to dice and card. It pleases them to trifle with the ordinances of God—why? Because they have other things to do. Oh consider, you that are self-pleasers, what a grievous evil you heap upon your own heads. You draw down more than swift damnation. How can this be? A man may heap up more than mere damnation—double damnation is more than single. Now if you please yourselves, live as you please, do as you will, you heap upon yourselves damnation with a curse. "The Lord knoweth how to deliver the godly out of temptations, and to reserve the unjust unto the day of judgment to be punished", (2 Peter 2:9). But especially he reserves certain kinds for the heaviest judgment—unclean persons, rebels against God, the presumptuous who build castles in the air on God's mercy, and, in the original, the self-willed (that is, the self-pleasers), those who follow their own will and pleasure. These are the ones God marks out especially to cast into damnation. This is to heap upon yourself damnation—and more than damnation.

And in this way, by God's assistance, you have seen the full prosecution of this point.

Sermon 7:
A Caveat Against Late Repentance

Luke 23:42, "And he said unto Jesus, Lord, remember me when thou comest into thy kingdom."

These are the words of the penitent thief upon the cross. Extraordinary cases *never* make a common rule. The ordinary rule is this: as is a man's life, so is his death. It is a common axiom, and as true as it is common: *Qualis vita, finis ita*—such as the life is, such is the end. A good life cannot but have a good death, and a wicked life a cursed end. This is the *ordinary* rule.

Nevertheless, there are extraordinary cases in which it may be otherwise, and these may be reduced to four heads.

First, when it pleases God to exercise his royal prerogative, he may convert a man at the last gasp, and give to the last even as to the first (Matthew 20:13). His grace is his own, Christ is his own, heaven is his own, and he may do with his own as he will. This is God's prerogative, as a king may pardon an old, beaten traitor to show his sovereignty. But this is *not* ordinary.

Secondly, when a sinner has had no means of salvation in his life, but only at his death—as when Paul came to Corinth, and many lay upon their deathbeds. Paul converted some of them (1 Corinthians 15:29). They had been pagans before, and never had the means of salvation until that hour. Yet so it pleases the Lord sometimes to step in and convert a sinner who never had the means before. But this case is not ordinary either; for now we have the means.

Thirdly, when God makes a sinner into an example to all the world—such as when a thief is brought to the gallows and there the Lord converts him. For all we know, this may have been the case of Achan (Joshua 7:25), who perhaps was converted when the stones flew about his ears.

Fourthly, when the Lord is as much honored by a man's death as he has been dishonored by his life. In such a case, God may give repentance at the end. This was the case of the thief on the cross; he honored God at his death *as much as many* who had lived their whole lives in *holiness*.

But mark this: the privileges of a few make no common rule. Men deal with repentance as they do with their wills—they put them off until the last gasp. So they put off repentance until the last hour, like Ahithophel, who never set his house in order until he went and hanged himself. As it is said of the serpent, it grows crooked all its days, and when it dies then it straightens itself. So many walk perversely while they live, and then, to straighten all, cry for mercy at death. Like the heart of oak, which never grows soft until it is dead and rotten, so they never soften their hearts with repentance until they see they must die. Then they fall to their beads and say, was not the thief converted at the last? Did not the thief on the cross find forgiveness? And why not I? In this way they lean on the thief's example. I dare say, that thief never stole more goods in his life than his example has stolen souls from heaven after his death.

Therefore, I have chosen this text, to show that the repentance of this thief was no ordinary thing, but an extraordinary wonder. And therefore, there is *no* trusting to it. For a man to live carelessly while in health, and hope to repent at the last, is a vain presumption.

That this thief's repentance was extraordinary I prove by five arguments.

First, because it was one of the wonders of Christ's passion. Christ's passion was full of wonders, both corporal and spiritual.

1. The first wonder was in the heavens. The sun was darkened, though the moon was full, which was a miracle in nature (Mark 15:33). This showed that Christ, the Sun of Righteousness, was eclipsed; for there was darkness over all the earth.
2. The second wonder was in the temple. The veil was torn in two (Mark 15:38), showing that the ceremonies contained within were abrogated, for the substance was present.
3. The third wonder was in the rocks. The hard rocks split, to convict the hardness of those who would not rend their hearts.

Sermon 7: Late Repentance

4. The fourth wonder was in the earth. "The earth did quake," (Matthew 27:51), to upbraid those who trembled not.
5. The fifth wonder was in the sepulchers. Many graves were opened, showing the power of Christ's passion.

And as there were corporal wonders, so there were spiritual wonders.

First, the centurion glorified God, saying, "Truly this was the Son of God," (Matthew 27:54).

Secondly, there was a wonder among the people. Beholding the things that were done, they smote their breasts and returned.

Thirdly, there was a wonder in this thief—for he was converted. "Today shalt thou be with me in paradise," (Luke 23:43).

In this way you see that Christ's passion was full of wonders, so that there is no ground for a man to delay his repentance, hoping to repent as this thief did, unless he also expects wonders. Can you look, when you are dying, that God will again rend the rocks, open the graves, or create new wonders? No, no—you cannot look for forgiveness if you defer your repentance. This thief's repentance was *extraordinary*, and one of the *wonders of Christ's passion*.

Secondly, this repentance was extraordinary in regard to its rarity. For among all men from the creation until that hour, it was never recorded that any one was converted so late as this thief. For all that we know, for this one thief who repented and was saved at the last, a whole world of the wicked who delayed repentance, living and dying in sin, were damned forever. For all that we know, Er and Onan, Jeroboam and Pharaoh—as they lived in sin, so the Scriptures plainly show they died in their sins. What need I speak of the hundred eighty-five thousand slain in one night (2 Kings 19:35)? What of the old world, who were disobedient in the days of Noah? They are now bound in chains. What of Admah, Zeboim, Sodom, and Gomorrah, burned with fire and brimstone? *As* they lived in sin, *so* they died and were damned in their sins, for all we know. Now what poor ground is this, for a man to defer his repentance and think to repent at the last hour, when among so many millions only this one thief found repentance? In this way you see his repentance was extraordinary, in regard to the number.

Thirdly, it was extraordinary, in regard to the *suddenness* of it. The work of repentance and grace ordinarily takes up the whole span of a man's life, and requires as many days as he lives. This is a great work, and it cannot be performed in a moment. Yet here, this work was attained while he hung upon the cross. And not for the whole time either—for the text says, "The thieves also, which were crucified with him, cast the same in his teeth," (Matthew 27:44). Both reviled him. Therefore, this thief was *not* repenting the whole time. It must then have been within the compass of one hour—or less—that this work was wrought.

Sermon 7: Late Repentance

Is it not a wonder if a man who knows nothing of music should learn that art in an hour? Or if a boy who cannot read a letter should, in one hour, learn to read, write, and speak good Latin? Or if an ignoramus should in an hour become a skilled lawyer? These are wonders indeed. And so, I tell you: repentance, grace, and conversion are harder arts than these. There is no art so difficult as learning the way to heaven. Can a man learn this in an hour? If he does, it is a *miracle*. David spent all his life at it. Timothy, from his youth, studied the Scriptures. Hilary said, "Ninety years have I been learning to die." If a man had the days of Methuselah, he could scarcely learn this lesson perfectly. Now, seeing repentance is so long an art, shall we think to repent as the thief did, merely because Philip was carried to Azotus in a moment (Acts 8:39), though it was some sixteen miles? Does it follow that another will be so carried? The way to heaven is long, and if the thief finished it in an hour, it was a miracle.

Fourthly, this repentance was extraordinary in regard to *its evangelical perfection*. Though it was sudden, it was not half-done, but complete, consisting of seven parts.

1. His penitential confession, as you read in verse 41: "We indeed justly; for we receive the due reward of our deeds." As if he had said: "It is just with God that I am brought to this gallows, and just with God if I were damned. I have spent my days roving, breaking God's commandments,

and now God has justly found me out." This was his open confession of sin.

2. His penitential profession: "But this man hath done nothing amiss," (v. 41). All Christ's doctrine was true, not one word out of place in all his life. There was nothing amiss in him. But the scribes cried "Crucify him" amiss; Judas betrayed him amiss; yet he is the Son of God. In this way the thief confessed Christ to be the Messiah and owned him against all the world.

3. His penitential satisfaction: As he had been partner with the other thief in sin, so now he labored to make satisfaction by seeking to turn him to God. Verse 40: "Dost not thou fear God, seeing thou art in the same condemnation?" As if he had said, "Alas, you and I have played the villains against God and are justly condemned. But as we have been thieves together, so now let us repent together, and call on God together." In this way he labored to convert his fellow thief.

4. Here is his penitential self-denial. He denies himself and loves the glory of God more than his own soul or salvation. Mark how he labors to convert his fellow thief and to make him give all the glory to God. He was so pierced in soul that his companion should dishonor God, that he sought to turn him before he prayed for his own soul. "Dost not thou fear God?"—this he spoke before he said, "Lord, remember me." He let his

own soul lie at stake while he labored to glorify God. It is plain, then, that he loved God more than his own soul.

5. Here you see his penitential faith. He believes, not with a general faith, but with a saving and particular faith. With faith and assurance, he looks on Christ as his Jesus: "He said unto Jesus." There is not one idle word in this text. The Holy Spirit says, "He said unto Jesus." It does not say he *thought* to say so, but he *truly* said it. The Spirit of God witnesses that he spoke directly to Christ as his Savior.

6. Here is his penitential resolution of newness of life and obedience for time to come: "Lord, remember me." He acknowledges Christ as Lord. As if he said, "I have followed the imaginations of my own will until now. All my thefts and sins have been to fulfill my own desires. But now I confess you to be my Lord, and if I were to live again, or any longer, I would forever serve you."

7. Lastly, here is his penitential prayer: "Lord, remember me." He acknowledges Christ as Lord. And not only did he pray in this way once, but—as Basil notes—he offered much prayer, as much as his short time allowed. These words are but the sum of his petitions: "Lord, remember me." Thus you see, he was no longer a thief but a convert and confessor. As Augustine observes, once a wicked thief stealing earthly things, now

a good thief breaking through into the kingdom of heaven—he stole paradise. Here, then, is a marvelous repentance: faith was in it, humiliation was in it, turning to God was in it, self-denial was in it, satisfaction was in it, and open glorifying of God was in it. Indeed, he was the only professor of Christ to the nations at that hour. None else spoke for Christ but this thief. None else stood for him but this thief. He was the only confessor of Christ at that time—the only man on earth then glorifying God. Therefore, unless you expect a death such as his, to bring such glory to God as this thief did, never rest upon his example.

Fifthly, this repentance was extraordinary in regard of its *incomparableness*. Never was there such repentance since the world began, nor shall be while the world stands. For when all the world—Jews and Gentiles—stood in obstinacy, priests and rulers, great and small, all crying, "Crucify him"; when the disciples doubted; this thief believed. When Peter denied Christ, this thief confessed him. When all the apostles fled, this thief stood his ground and maintained Christ against them all. When Mary Magdalene—out of whom Christ had cast seven devils—stood afar off, and the mother of Zebedee's children also stood afar off, this thief alone publicly acknowledged Christ as Savior of the world. At that moment, as even the Papists observe, God had no visible church on earth but this one penitent thief.

Sermon 7: Late Repentance

In this way this thief put to shame *all the world* for repentance—*even* the apostles of Christ. Now show me such a repentance as this, by which you may put Peter and all the apostles to shame. Either show such an extraordinary, incomparable, and wonderful repentance—or never trust in the thief's example on the cross. If a man had a hundred miles to go for his life, and but a short time allowed, he must run swiftly. Now the way to heaven is long. He who begins and ends that journey when he is dying must be the fastest runner that ever lived—this thief only excepted. If you run to obtain, you must have the art of prayer and repentance, or you will never overtake it, for it is far ahead.

Use. This serves to condemn those who rely upon this example. "Oh," says one, "did not the thief on the cross repent at the last hour? And is not God the same God still? And if he repented at the last, why may not I?" Many wrest this Scripture to their own damnation. They live in sin with the thief who went to heaven, yet die and are damned with the other thief who went to hell.

I will make this plain, because I desire to convince all who hear me.

First, when was this thief converted? Was it not when Christ hung on the cross? (Matthew 27:33). Christ then was to be inaugurated as King over all. And when kings are inaugurated into their kingdoms, they show that bounty then which they never show again all their reign. We have an example in the Chronicles of England of King Henry IV, who, at his inauguration, created fifty-five knights, hung all the streets of London with cloth of gold, and made the conduits run with sack, claret, and white wine. This he did at his inauguration, never afterward. So Christ, being inaugurated as King over principalities and powers, over hell and darkness, was pleased then to show mercy to this thief *to eternal life*. But as King Henry never repeated such bounty, so, *for all we know*, the Lord has never done the like before nor since.

Secondly, kings at their inauguration pardon certain offences, forgive wrongs, treasons, and felonies, which they will never pardon again. We read of Charles III of France, who on the day of his coronation pardoned all crimes against the crown. Why? Because he was crowned, and he would make that day a day of rejoicing. So Christ, when he triumphed over hell, forgave the sins of this thief—a pardon such as we never read of elsewhere, and for all we know shall never be seen again.

Thirdly, where was this thief pardoned? Was it not at Golgotha, where Christ was crucified, the very place of his triumph, his coronation, his victory, where he forgave transgressions and sins? There it was that Christ pardoned him.

Now, as it is with a captain who, when he has won the victory, sets up some monument at the place as a token thereof—so Christ, having fashioned the salvation of the world, set up a monument where he accomplished it. And none greater than this could be—not the rending of the rocks, nor the earthquake, nor any of the wonders besides so honored the death of Christ as the *conversion* of this thief. Like a physician who, having made an excellent medicine and being eager to test it, will try it freely though afterward he will not do so for much—so Christ, having made an admirable sovereign plaster for the salvation of mankind, as soon as he had made it, applied it to this thief. As if he had said, "Now you shall see what my death can do." In this way you see the conversion of this thief was not ordinary, but an extraordinary wonder.

Fourthly, consider how he was cured by forgiveness—not by bare repentance only, but by repentance joined with martyrdom. He did not only repent of his sin, but he died also as a martyr for Christ. Though at first he was hung on the cross for his evil deeds, yet afterward, when he repented and confessed the Lord Jesus Christ, proclaiming him to be the Messiah, condemning Pilate, Herod, and the Jews by declaring that he was unjustly crucified and that he was the Son of God, then his death changed its nature. At first they hung him for sin, but when he confessed Christ, they let him hang for his religion. For by their own law it was clear: whoever confessed Christ should be punished. Thus, confessing Christ, they let him hang as a martyr. And what a testimony he gave to Christ! "But the other answering rebuked him, saying, Dost not thou fear God?" (Luke 23:40). As if he said, "You see the scribes and Pharisees fear not God, they have conspired against the Son of God. The Jews who ought to have believed on him cry, Crucify him. Herod mocked him, Pilate condemned him. Do you not yet fear God? You who are under the same condemnation, about to be damned within the hour—will you not fear God?" Oh, what a testimony was this to Christ! No wonder he found mercy when the Lord so enlarged himself in bringing his soul to him.

[Objection] But it may be objected: Why is this Scripture recorded, if I may not use it to argue for late repentance, seeing all Scripture is written for our learning?

[Answer] The common reply is this: it is recorded once, that none might despair; but only once, that none might presume. Christ saved him at the last gasp, that when a man comes to that extremity he might not despair if he repent and become a new creature. Yet only one was saved at the last, that none might presume. There are also further reasons why this Scripture is recorded.

First, to show the sovereignty of Christ's death. As Christ in his life healed all manner of sickness, so in his death he is able to heal all manner of sins. It is the leaves of that tree alone which heal the nations (Revelation 22:2). Therefore, the Scripture sets down the desperate example of a thief. For what is more desperate than to be a thief? Christ did this to show that even to such he can show mercy—that all the world may take notice of the virtue of his death.

Secondly, it is recorded that no poor soul should cry out of his sins, saying, "I am damned, I am accursed, I am more sinful and graceless than any man." Do not reason in this way. Here is set down the example of a thief. And remember what Christ said to the multitude: "Are ye come out as against a thief with swords and staves?" (Matthew 26:55). As if he said, "You treat me basely, as if I were as vile as a thief"—implying that a thief is among the worst of men, even as bad as the devil (John 12:6). And it was counted among the great indignities against Christ that he was crucified between two thieves—the vilest sort. A thief, then, is the example of a desperate man. Yet see how Christ showed mercy to a thief. Therefore, if the Lord has enlarged your heart to repent, be not discouraged, but lay hold on Christ.

Thirdly, it is recorded so that we may not utterly cast off all men who come to the last extremity. Though great sinners, they must not be counted hopeless. Suppose a man has been a drunkard—yet prayer may be made for him, and God may open his eyes. There is still some possibility of salvation, though it is a thousand to one. Yet still there is some possibility, for one thief was saved at the last. Therefore, a drunkard, or the like, is not to be reckoned past hope. Though there are many improbabilities, yet we cannot tell but that this may be the second, to whom the Lord will give repentance. For this reason the Lord converted this thief.

Lastly, this narrative is recorded that we might be encouraged to believe and to turn early. For if the

Lord was so willing to receive the thief who sought him only at the last hour, how much more ready will he be to receive you, if you seek him while it is yet early? But as for you who persist in sin, and rest upon the thief's example, let me tell you: this story was never written for your comfort. The Lord knew how men would abuse it. Therefore Matthew, Mark, and John omit it. And if Luke had not recorded it, all the world would have thought both thieves were damned. Indeed, Matthew says "the thieves"—both reviled him (Matthew 27:44). Only Luke records the conversion of one thief, as if he were loath to leave it out, lest some poor soul should need it for comfort. But let me here strike off the fingers of all who would seize upon this narrative to delay their repentance. This example does not belong to you.

First, because this thief never had the means of grace before. Where do you read that he ever had? Perhaps while Christ was preaching, he was pilfering. Where do you read that he ever heard Christ, or the apostles, or the seventy, or John the Baptist? Nowhere. He wandered up and down in roving wickedness. We have not the least hint that he had the means of salvation before. But you—you have the preaching of the Word reproving you for your sins. And if you will still go on, you shall die (Ezekiel 3:19).

Secondly, this narrative does not belong to you. Where do you read that this thief ever built upon such a hope? Do you think he said, "I will steal as long as I can, I know I shall be imprisoned, and I shall be crucified

Sermon 7: Late Repentance

with Christ, but while I lie in prison I will repent, and then he will have mercy on me"? Did this poor thief ever dream of such hopes? Did he presume on mercy, and so sin against mercy? No. Therefore you who build on this example, whoever you are, it does not belong to you.

"Tush, tush," says the drunkard, "shall I be damned? The thief was saved." You cursed wretch! What if you should repent and cry for mercy? Are you sure the Lord will hear and pardon you? "When I spake unto you, ye would not hear, but rebelled against the commandment of the Lord, and went presumptuously," (Deuteronomy 1:43). Do you presume on God's mercy, that he will convert you at the last? I tell you, God's mercy is good mercy. It is not like the mercy of a wicked judge, who is wickedly merciful and lets rogues go free. No, God's mercy is good (Psalm 109:21). Mercy and justice are one with God, and in Scripture they share the same name. "Henceforth there is laid up for me a crown of righteousness, which the Lord, the righteous judge, shall give me at that day," (2 Timothy 4:8)—that is, the merciful judge. God is just in his mercy. Therefore, do you think to live in your sins, to swear, to lie, to be drunk, and yet hope for mercy? You are deceived. The Lord's mercy is just mercy, and he will damn you forever if you do not repent sincerely.

You never read in Scripture of mercy in the devil's ways. But, "All the paths of the Lord are mercy and truth unto such as keep his covenant and his testimonies," (Psalm 25:10). So long as you walk in the

Lord's ways, there is mercy in every step—mercy in prayer, mercy in hearing the Word, mercy in the sacraments. But in the devil's ways there is no mercy. As long as you walk in darkness, in presumption, and in sinful and vain courses, which are the devil's ways, there is no mercy for you. "They that observe lying vanities forsake their own mercy," (Jonah 2:8). You must turn from your own ways. For the way of mercy lies in another road—the road of holiness, humility, and repentance, the road of forsaking your vain imaginations. If you follow your own ways, God will have no mercy on you. He will not lie to pardon you. "He hath remembered his mercy and his truth," (Psalm 98:3). If you are a drunkard and die in that sin, God has said he will damn you (Galatians 5:21). He would be a liar if he did not. But mercy and truth are joined together in him. Therefore, repent in time.

"Pish, pish," says the drunkard, "I hope the Lord will be more merciful. These preachers preach nothing but damnation. I hope the Lord will pardon me." "How shall I pardon thee for this? Thy children have forsaken me, and sworn by them that are no gods: when I had fed them to the full, they then committed adultery, and assembled themselves by troops in the harlots' houses," (Jeremiah 5:7). As if God said, "I cannot pardon you. You will not come to me. You have forsaken me in my ordinances." Will a physician cure a man who will not come to him? "They have forsaken me," says God, "and they will not come to me." As if he should say, "I am

Sermon 7: Late Repentance

willing to pardon. I send out my commandments, but they will not bend their minds to keep them." Shall I have mercy on them? No, I will rather visit them for these things (Jeremiah 5:9). "He that despised Moses' law died without mercy," (Hebrews 10:28). How then will you expect mercy, who despise the *gospel* of Christ? The cross of Christ calls you. He woos you by his death and passion. If now you will not obey, you shall die without mercy.

Oh, what a cursed conclusion is this: "I have a merciful Father, therefore I will lift up my head against him. I know he will forgive me. I will break my head, for I know where to find medicine. I will wrong a man, for I know he will not sue me." You cursed soul! Though the Lord pardon ten thousand, he will not pardon you. No—you sin with a high hand. "Keep yourselves in the love of God, looking for the mercy of our Lord Jesus Christ unto eternal life," (Jude 21). Keep yourselves there if you are wise. For if God's patience is abused, it will be turned into wrath and wormwood, burning like fire unto the lowest hell. To the man who sins against mercy there is no redemption. This story does not belong to such.

Thirdly, this narrative is nothing to you because at that time God was in a way of working miracles. Then he rent the rocks, opened the graves, raised the dead. Unless you find God in that way again, never look to have your sins pardoned if you continue in them with a high hand. God may not be in that way of working miracles when you are dying. No. "To him that ordereth his conversation aright will I shew the salvation of God," (Psalm 50:23). Your life must be right, and your ways upright, if you mean to find mercy.

But the thief was converted without ordering his ways aright. I answer: one swallow does not make a spring, nor one fair day a harvest. One example does not make a rule. This example breaks no square. It is only he who *lives uprightly* who shall see the salvation of God—and no one else. If you mean to go to heaven, you must go by the way that leads there. There is but one way to heaven, and all who arrive there must walk that way. There is one faith, one new life, one kind of regeneration. God will have you go through all of these. You must run through every commandment. All who come to heaven must travel there. Therefore, never rest on this or that example. It was a wonder of wonders, one of the miracles of Christ's passion.

I remember the story of an ancient confessor, a worthy Christian who lived three hundred years after the apostles. This man had been a pagan all his life. In his old age he listened to Christ and said he would be a Christian. Simplinus, hearing him, would not believe it. But when the church saw him prove to be a true Christian, there was shouting and dancing for gladness, and psalms sung in every church: "Caius Marius Victorius has become a Christian." This was written as a wonder—that in his gray hairs he became a Christian indeed. So likewise, this thief's conversion is a great wonder and an extraordinary example.

Do you think there were not a thousand thieves at that time who lived and died in their sins, and so were damned? Were there not many widows in Elijah's days, yet to none of them was he sent but to the widow of Zarephath? Were there not many lepers in Elisha's days, yet none cleansed except Naaman the Syrian? So, there were thousands then, and yet, for all we know, they were all damned—this one thief only excepted. Will a man rush into a den of lions because Daniel escaped? Will a man cast himself into a fiery furnace because the three children came out unharmed? Will a man throw away his jewels because one among a thousand cast away his purse and found it again? No. These are wonders. Therefore, do not rest on this or the like example.

The common rule is this: *live in sin, and die in sin.* You that live in sin now shall be damned in sin forever if you do not repent. Paul knew this thief was converted, yet he said, "Be not deceived: neither fornicators, nor idolaters, nor adulterers, nor effeminate, nor abusers of themselves with mankind, nor thieves... shall inherit the kingdom of God," (1 Corinthians 6:9–10). Peter also knew this narrative, yet he said, "If the righteous scarcely be saved, where shall the ungodly and the sinner appear?" (1 Peter 4:18). James knew it too, yet he said, "Above all things, my brethren, swear not... lest ye fall into condemnation," (James 5:12).

This is a sweet example—if by it you return to God. But you make a damned use of it if by it you make yourself *secure* in your sinful course, hoping to be saved at last as this thief was. Consider: why did God give his commandments? Were they meant to be disobeyed while men live, and then, at death, to cry for mercy?

Again, why has God given you ministers to preach the Word of life? Is it only that they preach to men when they are dying? No. You must hear God's ministers while you live. Has God given you days to spend in sin? No. "I gave her space to repent of her fornication; and she repented not", (Revelation 2:21). God gives you time that you may repent. He could have sent you to hell at birth, but in mercy he gives you life and time to repent—that you might find forgiveness with him and become a new creature before you depart and are seen no more.

You who think to rest on the thief's example, take heed lest the Lord set you aside. Labor to obey while *it is still called today*. Use the Word while it sounds in your ears—before these things are hid from your eyes.

Sermon 8:
The Sovereign Virtue of the Gospel

Psalm 147:3, "He healeth the broken in heart, and bindeth up their wounds."

Here are two things in this text: the patients and the physician.

First, the patients: the broken in heart.

Secondly, the physician: Christ, it is he that heals and binds up their wounds.

The patients here are seen to have two maladies: first, brokenness of heart; secondly, woundedness—he binds up such.

Brokenness of heart presupposes wholeness of heart. Wholeness of heart is twofold: either wholeness of heart in sin, or wholeness of heart from sin.

First, wholeness of heart from sin is when the heart is without sin; thus the blessed angels have whole hearts. So also, Adam and Eve, and all of us in them before the fall, had whole hearts.

Secondly, wholeness of heart in *sin*. In this way the devils have whole hearts, and all men since the fall, from conception until conversion, have whole hearts. These are they of whom our Savior speaks: "They that are whole need not a physician, but they that are sick." The hearts that are whole need no physician, but the broken and sick do.

Sin is in the godly, and *they are sick of it*—just as poison in a man makes him sick, for it is contrary to his nature. But sin is in the wicked, and they are not sick of it. Poison is in the toad, and the toad is not sick, for it is of the same nature as the poison. In this way it does not need a physician. Will a physician go to cure a toad? Surely not—he will rather kill it than cure it. So, as long as a man is not sick at heart for sin, Christ will rather kill him than cure him.

If a man says he is sick, yet he can sleep, eat, drink, work, and look as well as ever he did—feeling no pain or trouble—what need has such a man of a physician? So also, when a man lives in sin, yet never loses sleep for it, but minds his pleasures and profits, never feels grief or anguish in his soul, he is soul-whole and heart-whole. What need has such a man of Christ? This is a man whole in his sins.

This wholeness of heart is called *fallow-ground* (Jeremiah 4:4). It is like an unbroken field, not tilled or manured; no harvest can come from it, for it lies unbroken. So there can be no harvest of grace in a man whose heart is fallow and unbroken. Therefore, to repent, to break the heart, is called in Scripture the putting of one's hand to the plow (Luke 9:62)—to plow up the fallow ground of the heart.

Brokenness of heart may be considered two ways. First, in relation to wholeness of heart in sin. In this sense, brokenness of heart is not a malady, but the beginning of a cure for a desperate malady. Secondly, in

Sermon 8: Virtue of the Gospel

relation to wholeness of heart from sin. In this sense, it is a malady, and yet peculiar to one blood alone—namely, God's elect. For though the heart is made whole, yet it is broken for sin.

As when a barbed arrow is shot into a man's side, and though the arrow is plucked out, the wound is not immediately healed—so sin may be plucked out of the heart, yet the scar it leaves is not yet cured. The wounds that remain under cure are the plagues and troubles of conscience, the sighs and groans of a soul hungering after grace, the stinging poison left by the blow of sin. These are the wounds.

Now the heart is broken three ways.

First, by the law. As it breaks the heart of a thief to hear the sentence of the law that he must be hanged for robbery, so it breaks the heart of the soul to hear the sentence of God's law: "Thou shalt not sin; if thou dost, thou shalt be damned." If ever the heart becomes truly sensible of this sentence, "Thou art a damned man," it cannot stand but must break. "Is not my word like a hammer that breaketh the rock in pieces?" (Jeremiah 23:29). That is, is not my law like a hammer? Can any rock-heart stand unbroken beneath its blows? Yet thus far a man may be broken and still be a reprobate. For all in hell shall be broken in this way, and therefore this breaking alone is not enough.

Secondly, the heart is broken by the Gospel. If ever the heart comes to feel its stroke, it will break to shatters. "Rend your heart, and not your garments, and turn unto the Lord your God: for he is gracious and merciful," (Joel 2:13). When all the beams of God's mercy fall upon the soul, they all cry, "Rend!" The heart cannot stand out if it once feels them. Beat your soul upon the Gospel; if anything under heaven can break it, this is the way.

Aristotle observes that a hammer may more easily break a hard stone upon a soft bed than upon an anvil. If you lay the stone on an anvil that will not give, strike as hard as you will with the hammer, it will not break into shatters—the anvil props it from falling apart. But if you strike it against a soft bed, it breaks to pieces. So it is with the soul. Preach the law as much as you will—preach hell and damnation, let that be the hammer—but then be sure to lay the soul on the Gospel, strike it there, and then it will break. If you smite a stone between hammer and anvil, though its parts might fly apart, they are stopped from doing so; the hardness on both sides holds it fast. So it is with the soul when struck with the wrath of God under the law: terror on the one side, fear on the other—yet the heart does not break. The soul knows not what to do. But smite it on the Gospel, and this, with the law, breaks it indeed. In this way Joel preached judgment and wrath to the Jews, but he laid their hearts upon mercy, and then the hammer cried, "Rend!" For he is merciful. He laid them on the soft bed of the Gospel, and then smote them.

Thirdly, the heart is broken by the skill of the minister in handling both the law and gospel. God gives him wisdom to press the law home, and understanding how to apply the gospel; by this means God breaks the heart. For though the law is a good hammer, and the gospel a soft bed, yet if the minister does not lay the soul upon it rightly, the heart will not break. He must fetch a full blow with the law, and set the full power of the gospel behind the soul—or else the heart will remain whole.

Aristotle makes another observation: lay an axe upon a block, and set a mighty weight on it, yet it will not enter to cleave the wood. But lift up the axe and fetch a full stroke, and immediately it enters. So also with the minister—if he does not have skill to fetch a dead blow at the heart, he may labor long and never break it. But if he strikes home, then, if ever, the heart breaks. "And I took unto me two staves; the one I called Beauty, and the other I called Bands; and I fed the flock," (Zechariah 11:7). There is the pattern of a true shepherd: he feeds with both law and gospel. He takes up his two staves and lays about him until the hearts of his hearers feel the stroke. This is the way to feed them, and to break them off from their sins.

In this way you see the means God uses to break your hearts. "He healeth the broken in heart." From this observe: Christ justifies and sanctifies—for that is the meaning.

First, because God has given Christ grace to practice for the sake of the brokenhearted. If his calling is to heal them, surely he will heal them. "The Spirit of the Lord is upon me, because he hath anointed me to preach the gospel to the poor; he hath sent me to heal the brokenhearted," (Luke 4:18). If he is appointed master of this art, even for this very purpose, then without doubt he will do it—and none else. He is not like Hosander and Hippocrates, of whom the story runs that their father appointed one to be a physician for horses and he turned to men, and the other to men but he turned to horses. Not so with Christ. No, he will heal those whom he was appointed to heal. And God appointed him to heal you who are broken in heart; therefore he will do it.

Secondly, because Christ has undertaken to do it. When a skilled physician has taken a case, he will surely labor to accomplish the cure. True, sometimes earthly physicians fail. Trajan's physician failed him, and on the emperor's tomb it was written: *Here lies Trajan, who may thank his physician that he died.* But if Christ undertakes the cure, you may be certain of it. He tells you, who are broken in heart, that he has already undertaken it. He has felt your pulse. "For thus saith the high and lofty One that inhabiteth eternity, whose name is Holy; I dwell in the high and holy place, with him also that is of a contrite and humble spirit, to revive the spirit of the humble, and to revive the heart of the contrite ones," (Isaiah 57:15).

He does not only undertake it, but promises to visit his sick patient. He will come to your bedside. Indeed, he will dwell with you all the time of your sickness. You will never lack anything, for he will be *ready* to help. You need not complain, "The physician is too far off, he will not come to me." He dwells in the high and holy place, yet he will come and dwell with you who are humble and brokenhearted. You need not fear, saying, "Will a man cure his enemies? I have been an enemy to God's glory—will he yet heal me?" Yes, if you are broken in heart, Christ will bind you up.

Thirdly, because this is Christ's charge, and he will look to his own calling: "To this man will I look, even to him that is poor and of a contrite spirit," (Isaiah 66:2). Mark that— "I will look to him," that is, I will tend him and keep him. Neither need you fear your poverty, as though you had no fee to give him; for you may come by way of begging, and he will look to you for nothing. "To him will I look that is poor, and of a contrite spirit."

Fourthly, none but the broken in heart will take physic of Christ. And this is a physician's desire—that his patient would cast himself upon him; if he will not, the physician has no desire to meddle with him. None but the broken in heart will take such physic as Christ gives, and therefore he says, "To him will I look that is of a contrite heart, and trembles at my word," (Isaiah 66:2). When I bid him take such a purge, says God, he trembles and takes it. I bid him take a bitter potion, or some unpleasant vomit, to drive him from sin; he trembles at my word, and dares not but swallow it. But when a soul does not tremble, the physician may say, "Let him be blooded," but he will not; he cares not for bleeding, he cares not for corrosives, he cares not for counsel, he trembles not at the word. Christ will never come at such a one. Christ bids you follow such a diet as to watch, to pray, to fast, to mourn, to keep in, to take heed to catechizing, not to grow cold through lukewarmness. If you tremble at his word, well. If not, but you will go on in your sins and be damned forever, then thank your own willfulness. But if you are broken in heart, Christ will assuredly heal you.

Suppose you should come to Christ, and his physic, though sovereign, is taken with a heart set against it. Then the physic cannot work. Imagination or fancy weighs much in the good or ill success of physic. If you carp at his precepts as too strict, or except against his word as if it had too much wormwood in it, if your imaginations run against his medicine, it will never cure you. Why so? Because you are not broken in heart to tremble at his word. But if you are broken, he will surely heal you. Then take his directions, though he should prescribe you to eat your own dung and drink your own urine—whatever he commands, take it, and I will warrant you health.

[Objection] But I have but a little faith.

[Answer] So had Peter: "O thou of little faith, wherefore didst thou doubt?" (Matthew 14:31). There is a little faith, and there is a great faith. "O woman, great is thy faith," (Matthew 15:28). Whether little or great, so it is true saving faith, it is good medicine, and it will assuredly cure. It is not the quantity of faith that saves a man, but the *quality*. True, a greater measure of faith, having more of the truth of faith in it, heals more strongly and steadily. But faith, whether much or little, if it is true, does the deed. Shall the patient doubt of his recovery because the physician prescribes but *a little*? He gives but a dram of powder, when perhaps the patient would have a pound. Yet the physician knows his art, and observes his measures—so many ounces of this, so many scruples of that. The skill lies in the measure. So, there is "the measure of faith" (Romans 12:3): one man has more, another less. Abraham had more than Lot, because Lot's soul could not bear so much as Abraham's. One of Hippocrates' aphorisms is this: Not too much at once. It is dangerous to empty the body all at once, or fill it all at once, or heat it or cool it all at once. The safest way is by little and little. So, God deals with you—now he gives some faith, and then a little more.

[Objection] But my faith is smothered; how then can I expect to be healed?

[Answer] A man is sick, and *violets* will cure him. The physician makes a compound with violets so that the leaves do not appear—only their virtue in the oil. Will the patient argue, "I cannot see a violet leaf, nor even the color; therefore it will not heal me"? No. So God gives many a soul *unguentum fidei*—the ointment of faith. The soul may not see one jot of faith in itself, yet it shall be cured, for faith is there in the compound. You weep, mourn, doubt, and complain that you cannot believe. Yet you never cease crying, "My God, my God." Well, here is faith in a mixture, though so compounded with other ingredients you cannot perceive it. There is faith so great that it flames out, and faith so small that it only smokes. But whether your faith is a flaming faith or a smoking faith, be of good comfort—you shall be healed. "A bruised reed shall he not break," (Matthew 12:20).

[Objection] But I am broken all to shatters, and I have no faith at all. How then can I hope to be cured?

[Answer] As your heart may be broken and yet be a right heart, so your faith may be broken and yet true faith. Sometimes it is bound up whole, sometimes broken all to pieces. A man that is broken in heart may not have faith gathered in one whole act, yet he has it in broken parts. Not one part is missing, though no part closes with another. The whole act of faith is this: *I believe that God is my God in Christ.* You may not have it in this way in one, but if you are broken in heart, you have it so in pieces.

First, you believe that God is God—there is one piece.

Secondly, you believe that to whomever God is God, it is only through Christ.

Thirdly, you believe that he who truly repents may say that God is his God in Christ.

Fourthly, you believe that repentance is a true hatred of sin as sin.

Fifthly, you believe—and your conscience tells you it is so—that you hate sin, not only as it damns, but as it dishonors God.

These are the parts of faith in its entirety. You have all the parts, though not bound up in one whole. In this way you have true faith, if you are broken in heart. *Totum non differt realiter a partibus simul sumptis* (The whole does not differ really from all the parts taken together), the philosopher says. He who has three groats cannot complain that he lacks a shilling. He who has ruff, stock, and string cannot be far from having a band. So, if you have faith in its parts, you have faith in the whole, though it may not yet appear entire.

Aristotle asks whether the parts are before the whole, as whether a man or a finger is first. I will not settle the question here. But this is certain: the *whole* is a relative thing, spoken with respect to its parts. First, we say that a whole is that which consists of parts, and then that the parts make up the whole. Therefore, if you believe in part, you truly believe.

In this way David believed in part. "Have mercy upon me, O Lord, for I am in trouble: mine eye is consumed with grief, yea, my soul and my belly," (Psalm 31:9). "For my life is spent with grief, and my years with sighing: my strength faileth because of mine iniquity," (v. 10). "I am forgotten as a dead man out of mind: I am like a broken vessel," (v. 12). David was a vessel of election, yet a broken vessel. He could not believe in the whole, for he feared God had cast him away like a dead man. Nevertheless, he was a believer in part—God's broken vessel.

[Objection] But I am sure I have no faith. I go weeping and mourning, I look on my sins with horror, I look on Christ with horror. I have not a grain of faith. How then can I be healed?

[Answer] Do you have a settled resolution to seek after God, come what may? Do you long to be united with Christ? Then, though you have no faith yet in act, you have something that secures you from wrath. There is a difference between *fides creditura* and *fides credens*—faith about to believe, and faith that already believes. It is actual believing that saves a man. But believing about to believe keeps a man from being a reprobate.

Though the child in the womb is not yet quickened with a reasonable soul, yet it grows and feeds there with only natural life, no more than what may be in a beast. Still, because it is in the making of a man, the mother does not fear she has a beast in her womb; she waits for God to give it a soul. It is secure from being a beast, for it has the dispositions that will not long be without the soul of a man.

So with many poor souls—too hasty in censuring themselves. Grant you have no faith as yet. Yet if you are broken in heart, you are about to have faith. Only let the word have its full work in you, to which you must diligently attend, and this *fides in fieri* (faith in the making) will soon be *fides in factum esse* (faith accomplished).

In this way the blind man in the Gospel was about to believe before he believed. He was no believer yet, for he had no faith; nor an unbeliever, for he was about to believe. "Dost thou believe on the Son of God?" Jesus asked (John 9:35). He answered, "Who is he, Lord, that I might believe on him?" (v. 36). As if he had said: Believe? Yes, with all my heart. Who is he? Where is he? I have been hated for his sake, I have been cast out for his sake, and I long to believe. Who is he? And when Jesus said, "Thou hast both seen him, and it is he that talketh with thee," (v. 37), then he believed. Chrysostom observes that this blind man was *about* to believe before he believed; he desired it in his soul.

So it may be with you. You ask, "Do I believe in Christ? Who is he? Where shall I find him in me, that I may believe?" You weep, hunger, and thirst after Christ, but cannot find him. You seek him in the Word and in prayer, but cannot yet see him. Yet your soul says, "I would believe with all my heart if only I could find him." In this way you may be about to believe, though not yet actually believing. If you have gotten thus far—about to believe—be not dismayed. The plaster is come, and it will heal you.

Understand my words rightly. A speech is not what it is taken for. I mean only *the broken* in heart. For otherwise, a man may be about to believe and yet never believe; about to be healed, and yet never healed. Like the wretch Zophar describes: "When he is about to fill his belly, God shall cast the fury of his wrath upon him, and shall rain it upon him while he is eating," (Job 20:23).

There is a twofold "about to be." First, such a thing as is about to be, and that is its very nature—it will never be otherwise, but always only about to be. Secondly, such a thing as is about to be, and that is its progress—not to rest there, but at last to be indeed.

Fear then, all you that are vain and yet in your sins. You are about to believe, but that is only the nature of your faith—it is merely about to believe, like the officers of the next year who are about to be officers, yet are not. Beloved, never expect to be healed unless you are broken in heart. You may be broken from some sins, but if not from all, it is nothing—you cannot be healed. Alas, you may be broken in some sense and yet never be healed. There is a double breaking, says Aristotle: either breaking into great parts, as wood into logs, or breaking into small parts, as stone into powder. Your stony heart may be broken into lesser stones—you may fall from greater sins to lesser, from drunkenness and riot to mere sipping, from open Sabbath-breaking by gaming to common talk of worldly affairs on the Sabbath, from never praying to cold and lifeless praying. Alas, alas, you still have a hard heart! When a great stone is broken into lesser stones, the little stones are as *hard* as the great one. Your heart must be broken to powder, if ever God will heal you.

First, because medicine never cures a man unless it can enter and run into the veins. When it enters the body and spreads through all the diseased parts, then it heals. But if the heart is not broken, the medicine cannot enter. Give a purgation to a stone: it may moisten the outside, but cannot soak in to soften it, because it is solid. But if the stone were powdered, then it would soak in even to the heart of the stone. God opened Lydia's heart, and *then* the word entered (Acts 16:14). Brethren, you have been under the hands of Christ's physicians ever since you were born. But where is the heart that is broken? All the medicine has been lost—the word has no entrance. It has skinned the wound, seared the outside, but the hardness of the heart remains uncured. How long have you been under medicine for curing your earthliness and vanity? How long under the means for your anger and malice? Yet never the nearer. Where are the broken hearts? I fear the medicine has not soaked—it goes no deeper than the surface. "The Lord is nigh unto them that are of a broken heart," (Psalm 34:18). Why? Because their hearts are open and broken, and Christ and his word come near—even to the quick. But if you are not broken in heart, no balm, no medicine can ever reach to cure you.

Secondly, you can never be cured unless *Christ* cures you. And Christ will never take you in hand unless you are broken in heart. A physician will not meddle with a desperate case that is incapable of medicine. Hippocrates says, *Let no physician set upon a fruitless cure.* It is fruitless to give you medicine, to pour in grace, to promise pardon, so long as you are *unbroken* in heart.

Therefore, Christ scorns to take you in hand. True, if you were broken in heart, God would not despise you: "The sacrifices of God are a broken spirit: a broken and a contrite heart, O God, thou wilt not despise," (Psalm 51:17). But if your heart is not broken, it is incurable. Indeed, if we consider Christ's absolute power, no heart is beyond cure—he can heal whatever it be. But God does not work by absolute power, but by the method set down in his word. And his order is this: first the heart must be broken, and then it may be healed. So long then as you are unbroken, you are incurable.

Thirdly, suppose Christ should begin to heal you, yet if you are not broken in heart, you will always be pulling the plaster off before the cure is complete. Sometimes God lays on the law and terrifies you, but then you tear off that plaster. You are like a dainty lady, who having taken medicine, and feeling it begin to stir in her stomach, thrusts a feather down her throat to vomit it up before it can work. Many do this—snatching at comforts and promises before the appointed time. In some physic, a quarter hour's difference may cost a man his life. When a patient is to be cut for the stone, and is bound hand and foot, if he but stir or struggle before the surgeon has finished, it is a thousand to one he dies. So, they in the second Psalm had a stone *in the heart*. Christ would have cut them, but they would not be bound. "Let us break their bands asunder, and cast away their cords from us," (Psalm 2:3). They could not *endure* their cutting. Men cannot be smitten at a sermon but they must *instantly* have comfort. As soon as the medicine begins to ache the head, sicken the stomach, and make the man very ill, it is then a sign the physic begins to work. But if he schemes to vomit it up, or purge it away, he loses all the benefit. Keep the plaster on as long as you can, if you ever mean to be healed. If the wound is thoroughly whole, the plaster will fall away of itself. But if you keep snatching it off, it will never do you good. If God has shot an arrow into your heart, bind the plaster close to the sore and let it remain until the venom is drawn out.

But if you are not broken in heart, it is vain to minister anything to you. You will not endure the medicine within, nor suffer the pangs you must endure if ever you are healed. Therefore, all you who are in any measure or manner broken in heart, be of good cheer. The Lord will heal you. "He healeth the broken in heart." See here these particulars.

First, for the seasonableness of it. The time to be healed is when the heart is in need, and the heart is in need when it is broken. As a man needs food when he is hungry, so a man needs Christ when his heart is broken. God will give what is needed, and in due season, says Augustine. "In an acceptable time have I heard thee," (Isaiah 49:8). God looks when it will be most seasonable to give grace, and then he gives it. Therefore wait, and never complain if God delays his hand. If he does, it is only for a better season. You say, "I need healing already." If God does not yet heal you, it is because the time is not yet seasonable. And the more need you are in, the sweeter the help will be when it comes.

Secondly, for the profitableness of it. When the heart is broken, then it will do good to be healed. But if God healed you before, it would hurt you. When the corrosive has eaten out the disease, then the cordial will help; but if the physician should give the cordial first, it would only feed the disease and endanger the man. So, many souls have been damned by catching at comforts before the corrosive has had its full work. You long for comfort too soon—what? Before sin is eaten out? Then you wish for your own poison. If God makes you wait for healing, it is for your good. Let his corrosives work their course, and then he will heal. "Wait on the Lord: be of good courage, and he shall strengthen thine heart: wait, I say, on the Lord," (Psalm 27:14). Never give up waiting, however long, and he will surely heal you when it is best for you.

Thirdly, in *puncto*—even in the very nick of your brokenness of heart—his healing will come. It is well noted that in the original, the word is set indifferently to any time, whether past, present, or to come. He does not fix a time, because he will do it punctually, just at the pinch, when you are broken in heart. Oh, then if you are not yet healed, know this—you have not yet come to that point. But when you are brought to it, you shall be healed.

What if you lie long under the heavy hand of God? Do not shake it off, but kiss the rod and humble yourself *more*. Sometimes God will not let a broken heart shake off his hand too soon. David would gladly have done so, but could not: God would not let him. "O Lord, rebuke me not in thy wrath: neither chasten me in thy hot displeasure. For thine arrows stick fast in me, and thy hand presseth me sore," (Psalm 38:1-2). David plucked and tugged at the arrows, but they stuck fast. He rubbed and shook to get God's hand off, but it pressed him still. It is needful that sometimes God's people should bleed long under his wrath, for by this the corruption of sin is purged.

So, with others—if they will scrape for comfort too soon, God *lets them*. But the result is this: the wound is only skinned over. Later it breaks open again, and they may lie seven years, sometimes twenty, sometimes thirty, with *no* comfort. All because they were too hasty. If they had been humbled thoroughly at the first, they might have escaped this long scourging. Now they repent of it every vein of their heart, and can scarcely claw it off *until death*. Yet such are still God's children, for they continue crying after him under all their misery. This is the very evidence that they are his. If they were reprobates, they would either sink into a fool's paradise of presumption, or else into a dead despair, never caring to seek God in his ordinances.

Therefore, beloved, do not pluck out God's arrows too soon. I do not speak this to all, for some will not pluck them out when they should. But I speak to those who are too hasty, who crave cordials before the corrosive has had its course. Some are but half-humbled, half-broken. As soon as they are touched a little, they think themselves thoroughly humbled. The heathen could say, we are often deceived by seeming virtue. Many think they are broken-hearted, when their hearts are only broken by halves.

It is as with a stick half in the water and half above—it looks bent, as though broken. But if wholly in or wholly out, it would appear straight as it is. So many are half in their sins, half out, and they seem to themselves broken-hearted, when indeed they are not.

But, beloved, before I give you the healing in this text, it is fitting to examine whether you are truly broken in heart. *Prognostica praecedunt therapeuticen*, says Argastus—*signs and symptoms must be noted before healing is applied*. Do you say you are broken in heart? Then it must appear by signs. If your carriage is mortified—there is a sign. If your communication is heavenly—there is a sign. If your companions are holy—there is a sign. If a man cannot discern you on this fashion, you are not broken in heart. Therefore, I will set down for you the signs and symptoms of a broken heart, that you may examine yourselves.

The signs I reduce to these two heads.

First, a breaking from sin, as a rotten member is broken from the body. The heart is truly broken when it is broken off from sin.

Secondly, a breaking in itself. The heart is broken when it is crushed with sorrow and self-denial, so that nothing can piece it together again but the favor of God.

These two make up a broken heart, and therefore they shall be the heads of examination.

First, then—do your sins go thick away from you? When a cold is once broken, we say, "Now it is going away," not thinly in rheum as before, but in thick phlegm. So, if your heart is broken, then your pride, your earthliness, your self-love, your deadness to good duties, and all your sins go thick from you. You may have some pores in your heart and your sins may fall thinly away as in rheum. But if they do not go thick away, the cold of your frozen heart is not yet broken.

Zacchaeus's sins were injustice and oppression. But as soon as ever his heart was broken, his sins went away thick—not dripping, as though he were loath to part with them, but in great flakes. "And Zacchaeus stood, and said unto the Lord; Behold, Lord, the half of my goods I give to the poor; and if I have taken any thing from any man by false accusation, I restore him fourfold," (Luke 19:8). See how his sins ran thick away—every word voided thick phlegm.

First, he *stood.* Before, he climbed and gazed after Christ; but being broken in heart, he stood ready, pressed to do whatever Christ would command.

Secondly, *he said unto Christ.* Before, Christ might have said what he would—what cared Zacchaeus? But now, broken in heart, though Christ had not spoken of such matters, Zacchaeus himself speaks to Christ.

Thirdly, *behold*. Before, his "behold" was carnal—he did what he did to be seen of men. If ever he gave, he wanted men to behold it. But now, his only care is that Christ behold it.

Fourthly, *I give*. Before, he thought, "I will give someday—I will give when I die; I will build hospitals when I am gone." But now that his heart is broken, he gives promptly.

Fifthly, *the half of my goods*. Before, he counted a penny or farthing to a poor body a great dole. But now, broken in heart, he gives half—not only of his superfluity, but even of his very substance. He gives not lightly, nor for show, but out of the very stock of his wealth.

Sixthly, *if I have taken anything wrongfully*. Though it is little, though from no great man but from any—rich or poor, young or old, stranger or no stranger—he restores. Not calling it a gift, as many do who cover restitution under the name of giving, but openly acknowledging it as restitution.

Seventhly, *I restore fourfold*. Before, he could swallow down his known wrongs. But now that his heart is broken, he makes amends even for the wrongs he only suspects he might have done. His restitution goes absolute—though his wrongs rest on "ifs," his restitution is certain, and that not niggardly, but fourfold.

So now he is broken in heart, his sins go thick away from him. The text called him "little Zacchaeus"

Sermon 8: Virtue of the Gospel

before he had seen Christ—*merito adhuc pusillus quia nondum viderat Christum* (rightly called little, for he had not yet seen Christ). But as soon as he saw Christ, whom he had wronged, and was broken in heart, he became a great penitent. His sins ran thick away from him. As soon as the boil is broken, out comes the matter; as soon as the vein is opened, out comes the blood—not a drop or two, but thick and full.

If you only pare off your sins now and then, your heart was never broken. For if once it were broken, your *reformation* would come thick and threefold. If we preach and exhort, and see only *thin reformation* in you, as a drop here and there, then your heart was never yet broken. If your heart is still full of self-love, pride, lusts, earthly desires, vain hopes, carnal fears; if your back is yet full of gaudy and foolish apparel—then your heart is not broken. Why? Because the foul matter still does not run out. Zacchaeus, when he was broken in heart, let his corruptions run out apace. His unreadiness for good duties, his deadness and dullness to holy duties—all were gone. Christ needed not to press him, for Zacchaeus himself spoke to Christ. His love of worldly credit ran out—for he gave half his goods to the poor. His backwardness and delay ran out—for he made present dispatch, "I give." His very secret and unknown iniquities ran out—"if I have taken any thing," *etc.* All his sins ran thick away from him. Why? Because a broken heart can hold no sin. This is the first sign of a broken heart from sin—that it is broken off from its sinful course.

The second sign is if it is broken from its wildness. The hawk is said to be broken when it is made fit for the lure. The colt is broken when fit for the saddle; but if it is not broken, it will never suffer the rider to mount. Man is born "like a wild ass's colt," (Job 11:12). So are you born, and so you remain unless broken in heart. If you are broken, then your heart is tame to every commandment, to every truth, and your affections are tamed to every precept. As Calvin puts it, *you are not yet fit for God's saddle if you let the devil, the world, or your lusts ride you.* You must be broken from this wildness, or you are not broken in heart. Perhaps you are bridled from some lusts, but still wild within. The beasts of Psalm 32:9 are bridled, yet remain stubborn. Do not be like horse and mule, as Ambrose says, who though they wear bit and bridle, would rather be at rack and manger, or feeding in the field, than bearing the saddle.

Do you despise to be curbed by the word, to be bitted by reproof? Do you long for freedom from restraint? God casts good motions into your heart, and you fling them off. God puts good purposes into your heart, but you will not fulfill them—like a wild horse that casts off his rider. You cannot bear a cross, but presently you are wild with choler and anger. Your flesh and blood cannot endure a touch, and yet you say your heart is broken? No—if you were broken in heart, every exhortation would tame you. You would love to be reproved and controlled by the word. You would leap at every commandment, however strict. But if you count holiness and zeal as mere "preciseness," you are but a wild colt still.

Look about you: many are like Ishmael, "a wild man," (Gen. 16:12). Wild in prayer, wild in hearing, wild in thoughts—their hearts gadding while the word is preached. Do you dare venture upon sin against the gospel of Christ and live in it till you are as a spiritual madman? The Psalmist compares such to Bedlams: "Why do the heathen rage, and the people imagine a vain thing?" (Psalm 2:1). Christ would have bound them, but they would not—"let us break their bands asunder, and cast away their cords from us," (Psalm 2:3). To swear, lie, covet, be drunk, break the Sabbath—this is madness, not liberty. Unless God breaks that wild heart of yours, you cannot be tamed. Perhaps you are restrained when temptation is absent, but if you are truly broken, you will refrain even under provocation. "I said, I will take heed to my ways, that I sin not with my tongue: I will keep my mouth with a bridle, while the wicked is before me," (Psalm 39:1). David bridled himself even when Shimei cursed him to his face. Here is the trial: can you bridle yourself when tempted? If broken in heart, you can. If not, you are still wild to this day. The wild beasts are tame enough till prey comes before them; so, you may be tame when temptation is down, but the test is when temptation stands before you. This is the second sign of a broken heart—that it is broken from its wildness.

The third sign: if your heart is broken, it is broken from pride. A broken heart is a humble heart. "To this man will I look, even to him that is poor and of a contrite spirit," (Isaiah 66:2). Pride is the root of all sin. Why does any dare sin? Because he thinks better of himself than he deserves. If a man felt that every sin makes him filthy—filthier than a toad—that every sin accursed him before God, he would not dare live in it. "Hear ye, and give ear; be not proud: for the LORD hath spoken," (Jer. 13:15). If the Lord speaks and you do not obey, you are proud.

You say, "I am not proud. I will hear the poorest speak. I will give all I think I can." Yes—but will you give everything to God? Is it not pride to go against God's commandments? He says, "Swear not," and you swear. He says, "Let not the sun go down upon your wrath," and you keep anger a month. This is execrable pride. You seek profits and pleasures *above* God's glory. One says, "I cannot live else." Another, "I cannot be merry else." Another tolerates sin in his house, "else I cannot live." You proud wretch! Must your mirth and credit lift their head above Christ's commands?

The word has not broken your heart until it has broken the neck of this pride. Do not tell me you are not proud in apparel. A servant may go in mean apparel, yet if he disobeys his master, he is proud. Do not tell me you bow to God in prayer. You may crouch, bow, and bend, and yet be proud if your corruptions refuse to stoop to his word. Until every corruption stoops to every commandment, your heart is not broken.

If you mock preaching as too strict, if you scorn zeal as "preciseness," your heart is unbroken. If ever you are Christ's, you will not only obey, but count it your honor to obey. David, broken from his pride, said, "Thou art my glory," (Psalm 3:3). He counted it his glory to serve God, his glory to be reproached for God.

We call *learning* or *wit* a man's "excellency." But holiness and zeal, men count no excellency. Yet I tell you: if you do not reckon it your honor to be forward for God, your excellency to lie in being godly and heavenly, you are but a proud fool. John Huss, when to write on James, trembled at his unworthiness, "*Hei mihi laudare te contremisco*"—ashamed at his vileness in so high a work. Such is a broken heart.

God is called "the excellency of Jacob," (Amos 8:7). It was not their valor or wisdom, but that God was their God. Your riches are proud riches if you prize them above God. Your obedience is proud obedience if you do not count it your glory to obey. This is the third sign of a broken heart—that it is broken from its pride.

Sermon 9:
A Funeral Sermon

Isaiah 57:1, "The righteous perisheth, and no man layeth it to heart: and merciful men are taken away, none considering that the righteous is taken away from the evil to come."

At the end of the former chapter the Prophet reproves the special sin of idol shepherds who followed their own pleasures and profits, not regarding their flock. Now he reproves the general sin of security in the people, namely this, that whereas the righteous perish, no man lays it to heart; and merciful men are taken away, none considering, *etc.*

This verse is a complaint of the Prophet concerning the people in general, for that they did not consider the judgments of God upon them in taking away the righteous from among them.

In the words themselves we are to consider: First, the work of the Lord, namely, the righteous perish and merciful men are taken away.

Secondly, the people's sin in not considering it, not regarding this work of the Lord, which is, that the righteous may be delivered from the evil to come.

By "righteous" is here meant not such as are legally righteous by the works of the law, for so no man is righteous, but by righteous is here meant such as are evangelically righteous, by the righteousness of faith in the gospel.

"Perisheth," that is, from the earth; for otherwise the righteous do not perish.

"No man considering," that is, no man lamenting, mourning, or grieving for the loss of them.

The first thing then to be considered is from the first part; and it is plain out of the words of the text, that *all* men must die, even the most holy and most righteous; for they are all subject to the stroke of bodily death as well as the wicked. "For there is no remembrance of the wise more than of the fool forever; seeing that which now is in the days to come shall all be forgotten. And how dieth the wise man? as the fool," (Ecclesiastes 2:16). "Your fathers, where are they? and the prophets, do they live for ever?" (Zechariah 1:5). So, we see prophets and fathers die as well as other men. Yes, those worthies recorded in the Scripture, Noah, Abraham, David, *etc.*, they all went the same way; they are all dead.

The first reason is because "it is appointed unto men once to die, but after this the judgment," (Hebrews 9:27). God has so *decreed* it, and therefore it must be so.

Secondly, because all men and women are of the dust, and therefore must return to the dust again. "In the sweat of thy face shalt thou eat bread, till thou return unto the ground; for out of it wast thou taken: for dust thou art, and unto dust shalt thou return," (Genesis 3:19).

Thirdly, because all have sinned, even the most righteous man. "For all have sinned, and come short of the glory of God," (Romans 3:23). Now "the wages of sin is death," (Romans 6:23). Therefore the most righteous man must die.

Fourthly, because as death came into the world by sin, "Wherefore, as by one man sin entered into the world, and death by sin; and so death passed upon all men, for that all have sinned," (Romans 5:12), so sin must go out of the world by death. Therefore, it is needful that the righteous die, that they may be freed from sin.

[Objection] But some may object and say, Has not Christ abolished death? Why then do the righteous die?

[Answer] I answer: he has abolished death as he has abolished sin. Now he has not taken sin completely away from us, for we see it still remains in us; neither has he completely abolished death from the righteous, for we see they all die. But he has abolished the dominion of sin, so that it no longer reigns in us; and so he has taken away the dominion of death, so that it does not rage as a tyrant over us, so that it is not hurtful to us as a punishment, but as a means to convey us into a better life. Christ has taken away the sting both of sin and death, though not the things themselves away from us; yet he will one day free us from them both. So, then the righteous must suffer death as well as the wicked, though not in the same kind.

Let no man then look to be exempted from death for his righteousness, nor from any outward miseries that may befall the sons of Adam. Indeed, if we are the servants of Christ, we must expect a greater share in these than other men: greater crosses, greater afflictions, greater sickness, and harder pangs of death often befall the righteous, as it did unto this our brother, who though he was old and stricken in years, yet the pangs of death were strong upon him. Those whom God will make heirs of eternal life, he allows them to have a greater portion in these afflictions. But the wicked are fat and full, and die with their bones full of marrow, as Job speaks; they commonly have little sickness and an easy death. But the godly do ordinarily undergo greater pangs. Let none therefore think that for his righteousness he shall be free.

Secondly, consider how few among us have learned this arithmetic, namely, to number our days, and they are but short, even a span long. Who is there that thinks of death? Who prepares himself for it? And yet all, even the most righteous, must die; for God has placed that fiery blade of death at the entrance into the paradise of heaven, so that none can enter before they taste of death, and all must taste of it. Yes, the most righteous are not exempted from the stroke of death. This then should teach us to labor to draw our hearts from the love of this present life. And what can better persuade us and wean us from the love of this world than a due consideration of death? We know we must all die, and therefore we should prepare ourselves for it. If any profane person among us knew that this night must be his last night, and that now he had no longer to live, would not this amaze him and make him think, and prepare for death?

If rich covetous men, who spend the whole course of their life in providing for the things of this life, truly considered death, and that their end draws near, would they do as they do, when this life and all the things of this life, and all their joys and pleasures of this world will shortly have an end? For when death comes, they will all be taken from us, or rather we from them. Oh how excellent a thing it is then for us to be drawn from the things of this life unto a due consideration of death, and of those heavenly joys and happiness to come! Oh you that look for these things, what manner of men ought you to be in holy life and conduct?

Thirdly, seeing we all must die, and this present life must come to an end, this should teach us to prepare ourselves for a better life, to provide for a surer building, a better estate which will never perish. Philosophers, who were but heathen men, could meditate on death, setting it always before their eyes. But this is not enough for us that are Christians. We cannot truly prepare ourselves for it unless we first build a surer foundation in providing for a better life, which will never have an end. And this no heathen or wicked man can ever do. Oh how woeful would that message be to a wicked man, that was brought unto good King Hezekiah: "Thus saith the LORD, Set thine house in order; for thou shalt die, and not live," (Isaiah 38:1). And why should it be terrible to him? Surely because he has no hope of a better life, he has not provided for a better habitation. Consider then with what comfort you could entertain this message.

With what comfort can you meet with death? For he is no Christian that cannot in some measure willingly meet with death, for by it we pass into a better life. For, as this our brother often spoke, he that would have comfort in death must look beyond death; he must not fix his eyes on the terrors of death, but he must look beyond to that glorious inheritance to which we are passing through death. And there he will behold his Savior putting forth his hand, ready to receive him. There he will see the blessed saints and angels whose company he will enjoy, besides an infinite heap of joys and happiness that is prepared for him also. O my beloved, nothing will make us willingly entertain the message of death but only the comforts of the life to come. Oh let us labor then for these comforts, that we may be provided against death. Would it not be foolishness for a man who, being a tenant at will, and shortly to be turned out of his house, never takes care for another until he is cast out of doors? Beloved, we are all tenants at will, and we are very shortly to be cast out of our dwelling houses of clay. And will we not provide for a surer habitation? Death is at hand, and our life must *shortly* have an end. Let us therefore labor to be assured of a better life when this is ended, so that with *comfort* we may meet with death.

Now we come to the second point which is here to be considered, taken from the complaint of the Prophet that the people did not consider nor lay it to heart, namely the death of the righteous. From this I note, that the death and loss of good men must be laid to heart as a special cause of grief and sorrow.

We ought justly to be grieved at the death of a righteous man when God takes him from among us. How did the Prophet Jeremiah and the people lament the death of that good King Josiah? "And Jeremiah lamented for Josiah: and all the singing men and the singing women spake of Josiah in their lamentations to this day, and made them an ordinance in Israel: and, behold, they are written in the lamentations," (2 Chronicles 35:25). So devout men made great lamentation for the death of Stephen: "And devout men carried Stephen to his burial, and made great lamentation over him," (Acts 8:2). So all Israel lamented the death of Moses: "And the children of Israel wept for Moses in the plains of Moab thirty days: so the days of weeping and mourning for Moses were ended," (Deuteronomy 34:8). And Joash the king of Israel wept for the death of the Prophet Elisha: "Now Elisha was fallen sick of his sickness whereof he died. And Joash the king of Israel came down unto him, and wept over his face, and said, O my father, my father, the chariot of Israel, and the horsemen thereof," (2 Kings 13:14). And therefore, we should lament and sorrow for the death of any righteous man, yet not in respect of themselves, as if their case were worse now than before, for they are now more happy.

But first, in regard of God's glory whereof they were instruments to set it forth; for since they were taken away, God's glory is impaired, because there are fewer left who truly serve and worship him. For as David says, "The dead praise not the LORD, neither any that go down into silence," (Psalm 115:17). So then, they being dead, do not praise the Lord among the faithful on earth any longer.

Secondly, in regard of the great loss that others have by their death, who have always received much good by them in their life. For the godly so order and conduct themselves in all their ways that they do good wherever they come. Therefore, when they die, it must needs be a great loss to such who, if they had lived, might have been bettered by them.

Thirdly, we ought to lament the death of the righteous in regard of the evil to come. For while they live, they are as a wall about us to keep God's judgments from us. "And he said, Oh let not the LORD be angry, and I will speak yet but this once: Peradventure ten shall be found there. And he said, I will not destroy it for ten's sake," (Genesis 18:32). "If there be a messenger with him, an interpreter, one among a thousand, to shew unto man his uprightness: Then he is gracious unto him, and saith, Deliver him from going down to the pit: I have found a ransom", (Job 33:23–24). "Run ye to and fro through the streets of Jerusalem, and see now, and know, and seek in

Practical Divinity

the broad places thereof, if ye can find a man, if there be any that executeth judgment, that seeketh the truth; and I will pardon it," (Jeremiah 5:1). So that if there had been but one righteous man among the people in that city, the Lord would have spared them even for that one's sake. And therefore the Lord, speaking of the righteous, says, "And I will fasten him as a nail in a sure place; and he shall be for a glorious throne to his father's house," (Isaiah 22:23). Oh consider then what a loss we have when the righteous die; we are likely to perish, when the nail that was in the sure place is removed, cut down, and falls. "In that day, saith the LORD of hosts, shall the nail that is fastened in the sure place be removed, and be cut down, and fall; and the burden that was upon it shall be cut off: for the LORD hath spoken it," (Isaiah 22:25). You therefore of this congregation, consider and lament for this your loss, in that this good man is taken from among you. For who knows whether God spared this congregation even for this good man's sake? For it is the righteous only that God respects, and for their sakes he will spare a whole people. Therefore surely, as Solomon says, "The righteous is more excellent than his neighbour: but the way of the wicked seduceth them," (Proverbs 12:26). Yea, though never so poor and despised in the eyes of the world, yet they are *precious* in God's account. "And they shall be mine, saith the LORD of hosts, in that day when I make up my jewels; and I will spare them, as a man spareth his own son that serveth him," (Malachi 3:17). So the righteous are God's *jewels*,

Sermon 9: Funeral Sermon

the excellent of the earth, precious in God's sight. And have we not great cause then to lament the loss of such?

Seeing then it becomes all God's children to lament the death of the righteous, oh how far are all such from the Spirit of God, who are so far from lamenting that, on the contrary, they rejoice at the death of the godly man because he stood in their way? They could not follow their works of darkness as they would, but he hindered them. He stood in their light; they could not run on in sin and wickedness, but he would be reproving, admonishing, and telling them of their faults. And this makes them long for the good man's end, and to rejoice in it when it does come. These do not consider that when the righteous are taken from the earth, then they lie open to the judgments of God. But as the Sodomites thrust out just Lot out of their city, so that God's vengeance might fall the sooner upon them; for until he was gone, the Lord would not destroy them. "Haste thee, escape thither; for I cannot do any thing till thou be come thither. Therefore the name of the city was called Zoar," (Genesis 19:22). Even so do these men desire to be rid of the righteous, and rejoice when they are taken from them, not considering that they are open to God's vengeance which hangs over their heads ready to devour them.

We ought then to be most grieved for the death of the righteous when any of the saints are taken away by death. Oh what a comfort is a righteous man to the children of God! What a feeling of grace is there in such a one! What comfortable words come from the mouth of such men! How full of comfortable speeches was this poor man, always ministering comfort to those that came to visit him! What a loss is this then to us! It is more than if thousands of the wicked had gone together. And shall we not mourn for the loss of such a one? If one of our family or friends die, we can mourn for them, and with good reason. And shall we not mourn for the loss of one of God's saints, one of the spiritual family, one of our fellow members?

In this then examine yourself how it is with you. When you hear of any of the faithful that are taken away, are you grieved for it? Do you lament and mourn for it? If you do not, surely you are no true Christian. For the children of God cannot help but lay it to heart and lament when any of the righteous are taken from among them. "And Samuel died; and all the Israelites were gathered together, and lamented him, and buried him in his house at Ramah. And David arose, and went down to the wilderness of Paran," (1 Samuel 25:1).

Now concerning the sin of the people in not regarding nor laying it to heart, this was a great sin of security in them, in that they, as it were, rested on their pillows and cried peace to themselves, notwithstanding God's judgments upon them in taking away the righteous and freeing them from the evil to come. We note that:

[Doctrine] When God will bring any great judgment upon a people or nation, he will *ordinarily* take away his faithful servants from among them, so that they may be freed from the evil to come. In this way good Josiah must perish in his young years, so that he might not be taken with the evil to come. "Behold therefore, I will gather thee unto thy fathers, and thou shalt be gathered into thy grave in peace; and thine eyes shall not see all the evil which I will bring upon this place. And they brought the king word again," (2 Kings 22:20). So when God told Abraham of the bondage and captivity to which he would bring his posterity, he said, "And he said unto Abram, Know of a surety that thy seed shall be a stranger in a land that is not theirs, and shall serve them; and they shall afflict them four hundred years; And also that nation, whom they shall serve, will I judge: and afterward shall they come out with great substance. And thou shalt go to thy fathers in peace; thou shalt be buried in a good old age," (Genesis 15:13–15). And so it was with the ancient father, Saint Augustine. When the cruel Vandals besieged his city, he prayed that the Lord would either take him away or cause them to leave the siege. And the Lord heard him, and took him away, and shortly after the Vandals destroyed the city. So Luther, writing upon this text, says that the Lord after his death would bring great affliction upon Germany, and two years after it so fell out indeed. In this way ordinarily God takes away his servants from the evil to come.

See here the mercy of God to his children, in that he takes them away from among the wicked. He calls them out of this world that they may not partake of the evil to come. Shall anyone then think it a curse to be taken away early, in his young years? No, happy is he that is taken away from these miserable and fearful times wherein the judgment of God, for our sins, hangs over our heads and is ready every day to seize upon us.

Secondly, seeing that God, when he means to bring any heavy judgment upon a people, does ordinarily take away the righteous from the evil to come, this shows that when the righteous are taken from among us, we are certainly to expect some judgment of God upon us. For these are they who stood in the gap and kept off the fire of God's wrath from us, so that it should not consume us. But now being gone, we lie open to the judgments of God. Therefore, when any righteous men are taken from us, the loss of them ought to drive us to repentance, unless God's judgments come immediately upon us and consume us. Therefore, we must forsake our sins and evil ways, and perform new obedience unto God. So he will be merciful to us; yes, he will be a shield of defense unto us, and a wall of fire around us, and he will turn away his judgments from us.

Beloved in the Lord, we are here assembled to perform this last Christian duty of burial to the saint of God now deceased, whose soul I am as *certainly* persuaded is at rest with Christ in glory as I am sure his body is in this coffin. When I consider those excellent graces that were in him—his great knowledge in the word of God, his love, zeal, patience, and humility; when I consider his excellent gifts in comforting, exhorting,

Sermon 9: Funeral Sermon

admonishing, with his heavenly gift of prayer, etc.—and withal consider that he was unlettered, he could neither write nor read, I cannot but call to mind that in Acts 4:13, where it is said of the priests and Pharisees, that "when they saw the boldness of Peter and John, and perceived that they were unlearned and ignorant men, they marvelled; and they took knowledge of them, that they had been with Jesus," (Acts 4:13). Even so may we know that this our brother had been with Jesus, not in the flesh, but in the Spirit, and that from him he received these things, which book-learning could never have taught him. For he was a good man and full of the Holy Ghost, as it is said of Barnabas. Truly verifying that of the Apostle, that God has chosen the poor of this world to be rich in faith (James 2:5).

He was a true follower of Christ, of whom it is said, "How God anointed Jesus of Nazareth with the Holy Ghost and with power, who went about doing good, and healing all that were oppressed of the devil; for God was with him," (Acts 10:38). So, this disciple of Christ did good wherever he came. How many *by him* have been stirred up, comforted, admonished, and quickened unto good duties, feeding them with the lips of knowledge who fed him with bodily food? How often have I myself through him, been stirred up to good duties? How often have I been refreshed and comforted in my heaviness by this poor man! So lively did he bear the image of God in him, that it seemed to me as if Christ Jesus walked in him alive upon the earth. How much true service, sincere obedience, fervent and faithful prayer had the Lord out of that poor cottage wherein he lived? If ever there was a true child of Abraham, and an heir to the promise, this was he. If ever there was among us a true Israelite in whom there was no guile, this was he. If ever there was among us a true Christian that shined as a light to those among whom he lived, this was he. If ever there was among us a poor man rich in faith, this was he.

In his life he was a pattern to all that knew him, so contented with his estate, so diligent in the duties of his calling while health endured; in sickness until death, while speech continued, so comfortable that I never came to him but I went away bettered by him. Oh, how did he exhort and stir up all those that came to visit him to hold out constantly to the end, to grow and increase in those good beginnings which they had made! How often and how excellently would he speak of the benefits which we have by Christ, even the pardon of sin—more like a divine than a common Christian—and so feelingly did he express the certain pardon of his own sin, even the sweet assurance thereof, that it did my heart good to hear him.

Often did he deplore the state of these evil times in which we live, from which the Lord has now taken him away. Often did he with tears bewail the state of this congregation, and their unfruitfulness under the ministry of the word. How did he even with tears pray for his enemies? He had some enemies, but they were did not like his own brand of piety, religion, and care to keep a good conscience but were made enemies to him. Concerning them I must say, that which without trembling I cannot speak, that as they refused his fellowship while he lived, and sought to thrust him from among them, so I fear that where he now is, they will never come except they repent. Oh, it is a fearful thing to hate a man for his religion and piety. But such was his love and compassion toward them, that he did often with tears lament their estate and pray for them.

At the mention of *death* he would still repeat the point not long since delivered, that *he that would have comfort in death must go beyond death*, even to that glorious inheritance to which we are passing through death. And never in my life did I ever see any man so comfortably and contentedly address himself to encounter with death as he did. "Oh," said he, "this is the time that I have long waited for." And as the pangs of death drew nearer, so he used the more comfortable speeches, saying with Paul, "For I am in a strait betwixt two, having a desire to depart, and to be with Christ; which is far better," (Philippians 1:23). "Now shall I see my sweet Saviour whom I have longed for." And when death was even upon him, he said, "Come, Lord Jesus, come quickly," (Revelation 22:20). And so, with admirable patience he endured the pangs of death. After prayer with him, when his speech began to fail, I exhorted him now to look up to his Redeemer, who was ready to receive him into his Master's joy. And I spoke something out of the

Revelation concerning the happy estate of those that die in the Lord, adding further that all this comfort we have by Christ. He answered with these his last words, which with much difficulty he spoke, saying, "Blessed be his glorious name, blessed be his glorious name." And therefore this faithful servant of Christ and heir of blessing gave up his breath in blessing God, and died praising that God to whose praise he had lived.

And what should I say more but as David said of Abner, "And the king lamented over Abner, and said, Died Abner as a fool dieth?" (2 Samuel 3:33). Did this our brother die as a fool, as a worldling, as a wicked man dies, of whom no reckoning is to be made? No. Precious is his death in the eyes of the Lord, and in the eyes of all that fear the Lord, and blessed shall his memory be. Yea, all that knew him well will call him blessed. And for my own part, as often as I shall think of his death—and often I must think thereon—my soul shall wish and pray, "Oh let me die the death of the righteous, and let my last end be like his," (Numbers 23:10). Amen.

Sermon 10:
The Signs of God's Forsaking a People

Jeremiah 14:9, "And we are called by thy name; leave us not."

Two things, brethren and beloved in Christ Jesus, are intended and expressed by the holy Prophet from the first verse to the thirteenth verse.

There is first a declaration of a judgment, and that is dearth or famine, from the first verse to the seventh.

Secondly, the sword is threatened to the thirteenth verse: he will send the famine, then the sword, and he will not be entreated.

Then in the eighth and ninth verses we have the importunate prayer of the Church to turn away these judgments. And the prayer is marvelously sweet, in confession, where they confess their sins and seek to God for help.

First, they desire God that he would not take his providence from them: "Why shouldest thou be as a stranger in the land, and as a wayfaring man that turneth aside to tarry for a night?" (Jeremiah 14:8). As if they should have said, it is marvelously strange that you behave yourself so like a stranger. You see our sorrows and do not help us; you perceive our troubles and do not regard us. It is strange, it is strange that the God of Israel stands as a man astonished; that you who have before received us should now stand as one amazed and astonished, as if you were weary of this your work and could do no more, as if you should say, Jerusalem cannot be saved and Judah cannot be helped.

Secondly, they desire that God would not take away his presence from them: leave us not to ourselves, they say; let us see your face. Though we die, yet let it be in your presence. Yes, though you do not help us, yet it does us good to look upon our Saviour, and you can help us. And therefore you see the arguments with which they press the Lord, how sweet *they are*:

First, you are the hope of Israel. Alas, if you forsake us, we are all lost. Our hope is not in the means only, but our hope is in you. Leave us not, for you are the hope of Israel. It is the task you have taken upon yourself; leave us not, therefore.

Secondly, you have made yourself a Savior, and now is the time of trouble, therefore now perform what you have undertaken.

Thirdly, you are in the midst of us, that is, you are a great Commander among us, always ready to help us. And will you now see us perish? You are nearer to us than the Ark in the midst of the camp: "And when the Philistines heard the noise of the shout, they said, What meaneth the noise of this great shout in the camp of the Hebrews? And they understood that the ark of the LORD was come into the camp," (1 Samuel 4:6). As if they should say, he lives in the midst of us, and will he not save us?

Fourthly, we are called by your name, and therefore we have interest in you. To whom should wives go but to their husbands? To whom should children go but to their fathers? To whom should servants go but to their masters? To whom then should we go but to you our God and Savior? Leave us not therefore, and we will deal with none but you.

Secondly, though God might leave them, yet they beg that he would not. That is the *Amen* to their prayers: though you stand and will not help us, yet let us die in your presence. And this is the great request of the saints: they desire not to be left of God, although God might leave them. From this learn that God might cast off a people.

Israel did fear it, and it is that which they prayed against, that God might leave them. I do not say that God will cast off his elect ones eternally, but those in outward covenant. See Isaiah 1:2–3: "Hear, O heavens, and give ear, O earth: for the LORD hath spoken, I have nourished and brought up children, and they have rebelled against me. The ox knoweth his owner, and the ass his master's crib: but Israel doth not know, my people doth not consider." And verse 7 shows the judgment: "Your country is desolate, your cities are burned with fire: your land, strangers devour it in your presence, and it is desolate, as overthrown by strangers," (Isaiah 1:7).

There is an *outward* calling as well as an *effectual* calling. God may reject, for "many are called, but few are chosen," (Matthew 22:14), our Savior says. My brethren, cast your thoughts afar off, and see what has become of those famous Churches of Pergamos and Thyatira and the rest mentioned in Revelation 1:11. And who would have thought that Jerusalem should have been made a heap of stones and a vagabond people? And yet we see God has forsaken them, showing us thereby that although God will never forsake his own elect ones, yet he may forsake such as are in outward covenant with him.

The Lord is said to *dis-church* or discharge a people, "Then said God, Call his name Lo-ammi: for ye are not my people, and I will not be your God," (Hosea 1:9). And, as I may so say, he sues out a bill of divorcement. As it was in the old law, they that had anything against their wives sued out a *bill of divorcement* against them, and *so does God*. See Hosea 2:2: "Plead with your mother, plead: for she is not my wife, neither am I her husband: let her therefore put away her whoredoms out of her sight, and her adulteries from between her breasts." *Lest I make her as at the first*, that is, as she was in Egypt, poor and miserable. As if God should now say to England, Plead, plead with England, all you that are my ministers in the way of my truth, and say unto her, let her cast away her rebellions, lest I leave her as I found her in the day of captivity and bondage under the blindness of popery and superstition.

[Objection] But how does God cast off a people?
[Answer] I answer, first, when he takes away his

love and respect from a people, and as his love, so the *token* of his love, which is his Word and sacraments, the means of salvation.

Secondly, when he takes away his providence. I mean, when he takes down his walls, that is, his magistracy and ministry.

Thirdly, when instead of counseling there comes in bribing; and instead of true teaching there comes in daubing with untempered mortar. "And now go to; I will tell you what I will do to my vineyard: I will take away the hedge thereof, and it shall be eaten up; and break down the wall thereof, and it shall be trodden down," (Isaiah 5:5). Or when the stakes grow rotten and are not renewed, then is God going away.

Fourthly, when God takes away the benefit of both these helps, they are signs of God's departure.

Use. May God un-church or discharge a people and cast a nation off? Oh, then let this teach us to cast off all security. For miseries are near at hand in all probability. When we observe what God has done for us, all things are ripe for destruction, and yet we do not fear it, but we promise ourselves safety, and do not consider that England is ready to be harrowed, and yet we cannot entertain a thought of England's desolation. When there are so many prophecies in it of its destruction, yet we cannot be persuaded of it, but in our judgments it must not be, it must not be as yet, as if it were impossible that God should leave England, as if God were a cockering father over lewd children. God may leave a nation, and his elect may suffer, and why may not England? England's sins are very great, and the greater because the means are great, and our warnings are and have been great. But yet our mercies are far greater. England has been a mirror of mercies; yet now God may leave it, and make it the mirror of his justice.

Look how God spoke to the people that bragged of their temple, Jeremiah 7:4: "Trust ye not in lying words, saying, The temple of the LORD, The temple of the LORD, The temple of the LORD, are these." But what says the Lord by the Prophet in the twelfth and fourteenth verses: "But go ye now unto my place which was in Shiloh, where I set my name at the first, and see what I did to it for the wickedness of my people Israel," (Jeremiah 7:12). Even so, England, you have the temple and the priests, and yet may not God, who destroyed Shiloh, destroy you?

Go to Bohemia, and from there to the Palatinate, and from there to other parts of Germany. Do but imagine that you were there, or do but mark what travelers say. God's churches are made heaps of stones, and those Bethels wherein God's name was called upon are now defiled temples for Satan and superstition to reign in. You cannot go three steps but you shall see the head of a dead man; and go a little further, and you shall see the heart picked out by the fowls of the air, or some other sad spectacle. And then surely you will say, *Tilly* has been here or there. Now are these churches become desolate, and may not England?

Go into their cities and towns, and there you may see many compassed about with chains of captivity, and every man bemoaning himself. Look under a tree, and there you may see a poor fatherless child sending out his breath and crying unto his helpless mother. Step but a little further, and you shall see the helpless wife, the sad wife, bemoaning her husband. And this is her misery: she cannot die soon enough, but she shall see greater misery. For either she shall (as she thinks) see her little ones dashed against the stones or tossed upon the pikes; or, if they live, then they shall be brought up in Popery, and then she weeps again, and thinks that if her husband is dead, it is well. But it may be he is upon the torture rack, or put to some other torment, and then she dies a hundred times before she can die.

In this way if you can set your souls in their souls' stead, and imagine you were in their condition, and say, may not this be the condition of England? And who knows but it may? Oh, my beloved, be not high-minded, but fear. For as we have God's bounty on the one side, so (for aught I know) we may have his severity on the other side. Do not prance then yourselves with foolish imaginations, saying, Who *dare* come to hurt England? The Spaniard has his hands full, and the French are too weak. But beloved, be not deluded. Who would have thought that Jerusalem, the lady city of all nations, where the tribes went up to worship, should become a heap of stones and a vagabond people? But yet you see it was, and is to this day. And I pray, why may it not be

England's case? Learn therefore, hear, and fear God, for assuredly God can be God without England's prosperity. Do not say, here are many good Christians. Do you think that God is beholden to you for your religion? Surely not. For rather, than he will preserve such as profess his name and yet hate to be reformed, he will raise up of these stones children unto Abraham. He will rather go into Turkey and say unto them, "Thou art my people, and I will be your God."

But will you let God go, England? Are you so content, and will you let Christ go and God go? Oh no, no; lay heart and hands upon him as they did upon Paul. Every one of you lay hold on him and say, "You shall not go from us, for we are called by your name, therefore leave us not." And for my part I will pray that he does not take his leave of us. Do you think that Rome will forsake or part with her gods? No, they will rather lose their lives. And will you let your God go, O England? Plead with your God and let him not depart, but part rather with your rebellions.

"We are called by thy name, leave us not." You see the Church is very importunate to keep God with them. They lay hold on God with cords of arguments: "O thou hope of Israel, do not leave us." They beset God with their prayers, and as it were, they watch him at the town's end that he should not go away, and they say, "You shall still abide with us." They are importunate that he does not leave them. Here *observe*:

[Doctrine] That it *is* the importunate desire of the saints of God still to *keep God present with them*.

They cared not so much for sword or famine as they did for the loss of God's presence. "O Lord, leave us not," say they; this was their prayer. And blame them not; for consider what a grief it is that God should stand by and not help them. Good Lord, say they, leave us not. We cannot bear to think that God should leave us, much less can we endure to feel it or taste it. In this way they did, and so the saints of God should do.

Exodus 33:14–15: "And he said, My presence shall go with thee, and I will give thee rest. And he said unto him, If thy presence go not with me, carry us not up hence." Alas, Moses might have gone upon fair terms. "You shall," God says, "possess the land in peace with prosperity." But what says Moses? Though we might have Canaan and all the delights there, yet carry us not there unless your presence go with us. This is the stay and the strength that he relies upon.

So, Psalm 80:18–19: "So will not we go back from thee: quicken us, and we will call upon thy name. Turn us again, O LORD God of hosts, cause thy face to shine; and we shall be saved." Here is a man, a David, a heart worth gold. He does not make many requests, but he comes home; he sues to the purpose: "Cause your face to shine upon us." As if he should have said, that is prosperity enough, for it endures forever.

But what is the presence of God? In a word, it is the particular favor of God which he expresses in his ordinances. It is all the good and sweetness that flows from the purity of God's worship, by which God reveals himself to us. It is not gold, wealth, nor prosperity that makes God to be our God, for there is more gold in the West Indies than in all Christendom. But it is God's ordinances purely administered that bring God's presence to a people. God forsook Shiloh because his ordinances were not purely kept there. When the people left the Ark, that is, his pure worship, then God left the people. When the Ark of God's presence was among them—the word in the purity of it—then his face was there, and there God was principally present.

It was here that Cain is said to be cast out of God's presence, because he was cast out from the Church; he was cast *out from God's ordinances*. If a people outwardly reform and sincerely worship God, they may remain. If Sodom and Gomorrah had but legally repented, they would have remained, they would not have been destroyed. And it is here that the saints are so urgent for God's ordinances in their purity. But the wicked say once a Sabbath is enough, and once a week is too much. By this we may see that England is ripe; is she not weary of God? No, she is *fattened* for the *slaughter*.

But it was not so with the saints and people of God in former times. It was David's great request, that he might dwell in the house of the Lord: "One thing have I desired of the LORD, that will I seek after; that I may dwell in the house of the LORD all the days of my life, to behold the beauty of the LORD, and to enquire in his temple," (Psalm 27:4). And Psalm 42:1: "As the hart panteth after the water brooks, so panteth my soul after thee, O God." He said his soul did pant for God's ordinances. Therefore you see that the saints of God are marvelously importunate to keep God in his ordinances.

[Question] But may not a man be saved without preaching?

[Answer] I answer, the argument is clear: the saints maintain God in his ordinances, the lack of which is under the *penalty of death and damnation*, because we have more need of God in his ordinances than of all the gold in the world. For all the gold in the world will not satisfy a hungry man. It is bread that he must have, because he has need of it. So, the saints have most need of God and of Christ. For though they have but ragged coats and their bodies pinched with hunger, yet God is he whom they stand most in need of.

In Psalm 73:25-26, David fretted at the prosperity of the wicked, but at the last he breaks off kindly, saying, "Whom have I in heaven but thee? and there is none upon earth that I desire beside thee. My flesh and my heart faileth: but God is the strength of my heart, and my portion for ever." As if he should have said, let them have what they will, I will have nothing but you. And why so? Because you are my strength and my portion forever. Mark, he says that God is his strength, yes, the strength of his heart, hereby showing that all the helps in the world cannot help the heart of man if God and Christ are wanting.

You might as well offer a weary man a journey to refresh him, or the air to feed a hungry man, as to offer riches, honors, and ease to help a distressed soul. These will never help a man. He may well *dote* upon them, but his soul and conscience will still be galled and troubled. It must be the God of peace that must speak peace to troubled souls. It must be the God of peace that must speak peace to a distressed soul, to a soul that is damned in itself. It is he that must say, "I will be the strength of their hearts, and their portion for ever," (Psalm 73:26).

No wonder then if a poor soul cries to God when, though the heart may be full and the body pleased with delicacies, yet the poor soul, for all it knows, must go down to hell. Oh then, beloved, if you will have safety, go where God is. For every good gift comes in with him. If once a man has got God into his company, he has all good things with him. God blessed Obed-edom's house for the Ark's sake. Now the Ark was a type of Christ, and where it came, many blessings came with it. Even so, when God comes unto a people, they are married unto him in righteousness, in judgment, in lovingkindness, and in mercies forever (Hosea 2:19). When a man is married to a wife, all is his. So, get Christ and all is yours. And then what would you have more?

God speaks to the rain, and it hears; to the corn, and it hears. But if you are in Christ, then hell and death are your servants. But those that have only outward things—profits, pleasures, or the like—they have their ruin unless they have Christ with them. Get Christ therefore, for if he is lacking, all outward and inward dangers befall that man or that nation. Woe be unto him or them that are without God. "Though they bring up their children, yet will I bereave them, that there shall not be a man left: yea, woe also to them when I depart from them. Ephraim, as I saw Tyrus, is planted in a pleasant place: but Ephraim shall bring forth his children to the murderer," (Hosea 9:12–13).

It is true indeed, *woe* be to that heart, county, or kingdom that God has departed from. When God, who is the God of mercies and all consolation, has departed away, who can but pity that soul, county, or kingdom who will not submit to God's peace, consolation, and salvation? When God departs, all miseries follow. For that man that makes no conscience of out-facing God in the congregation, mark what the text says: "But it shall come to pass, if thou wilt not hearken unto the voice of the LORD thy God, to observe to do all his commandments and his statutes which I command thee this day; that all these curses shall come upon thee, and overtake thee," (Deuteronomy 28:15). And when the floodgates are once up, then comes in all evils. And then they shall say, are not these things come upon us because God is not among us?

If therefore we would avoid woe and sorrow, slaying and killing one another; if the wife would not see her husband killed before her tender eyes, and the man see his wife snatched out of the world by the hands of wicked men, then leave not God, but hold him fast, and then evil days will depart from us. It is our holding of God that keeps miseries from us. Oh then, what shall we think of them that are weary of God, and that say to the Almighty, "Depart from us," (Job 22:17)?

[Objection] But are there any among us that are weary of God? I hope there are none such among us.

[Answer] I answer: you that are a servant, and reject the command of your master, in it you reject God. And all such as have a low opinion of the worship of God and the word of God, and think that prayer or preaching continues too long—I say, these men know not what they think or say, but certainly it is because they would be freed from the ordinance of God. Well, God will free you from them one day, I warrant you, and then you will be in a miserable condition. Oh, that you would pity your poor condition.

But you that are weary of God's ordinances and of his mercies, his presence and patience, know this: you shall be deprived of God's goodness, and your portion shall be with those that hate God in this life here; and after this life (if you dont repent) your portion shall be with them in Tophet, "where their worm dieth not, and the fire is not quenched," (Mark 9:44). And then your crying will not avail. God will be God over you in destruction. Yes, when he has spurned thousands and ten thousands into hell, such as you are, then you shall be the everlasting object of his never-dying wrath. Then, notwithstanding all your shrill cries, though you could be heard out of that dungeon, yet your help would be never the nearer, for God is God still.

I advise you therefore what to do while you are here in this life. Make your peace with God in Christ, and lay yourself low before him, and bear patiently his hand in his wrath which you have deserved. And mark what I say: you have deserved to be in hell a hundred times—that is the least. And therefore, be content with your condition, for you have chosen death rather than life. And God would wrong himself and you also if he should not let you have your choosing.

Will not these things move you, my brethren? It seems to me I see your colors rise—I am glad of it, I hope it is to a good end. You may be wise, and perhaps so wise as to choose life rather than death. Now the Lord grant it, for he does not delight in your destruction.

I will add one word more, to leave the more impression in your hearts. My desire is the health of your souls. Though my food seem sour, yet my mind is the will of God. You man or woman, that cannot endure so much preaching, but stand on thorns while it is preached—"Too much of one thing," you say, "is good for nothing"—you do as much as to say you will not have God with you. You will have a little of God, but you will have more of your pleasures. Is this your desire, your delight? Know then, whoever you are, that have an ill will toward God and his ordinances, and will not have the gospel in the purity of it, you shall have your desires. You say, depart preachings, and so it shall. You shall have your desires.

When you shall hear the trumpet sound, and when your ears shall tingle with the sound of war, then depart forever. You that are weary of God, get you down to hell forever. Fulfill your base lusts (then will God say), for I have fed you on earth this twenty, thirty, forty, fifty, yes, sixty years and upwards, and my mild word could not rule you nor prevail with you. And therefore now, you will go to hell, and there remain forever.

Think in this way with yourselves: will God serve me like this? Yes, that he will, for he has prepared a place for the *proudest* kings, princes, monarchs, captains, and so forth, that are or ever were in the world, if they will not be ruled nor guided by God and his word. "For Tophet is ordained of old; yea, for the king it is prepared; he hath made it deep and large: the pile thereof is fire and much wood; the breath of the LORD, like a stream of brimstone, doth kindle it," (Isaiah 30:33). The text does as good as say, *he delights to make bonfires about their ears.* And must this be the way to glorify God?

But some may say, Surely kings and monarchs are exempt, they need not fear that such torments shall come upon them.

To this I answer, that God will say to them, *Reign there if you will.* And then they shall know that there is a King that *laughs at their destruction.* Take notice of this, I beseech you, and reason so with your own souls: is he a good son that cannot endure the presence of his own father? Is she a good wife that cannot endure the company of her husband? And is he a good Christian

Sermon 10: God's Forsaking a People

that cannot endure the company of Christ in his ordinances?

This may serve to rebuke God's people for their *neglect*. You see the gospel is going, Christ is departing, he is going to seek better entertainment. (But I marvel you give no better attendance. I pray, listen what I say and have to say. Stand up and hear, and the Lord give you grace to believe.) I will deal plainly with you: as sure as God is God, God is going from England. Shall I tell you what God told me? Yes, I must tell you on pain of my life. Will you give ear and believe me? I am a poor ambassador sent from God to deliver his message to you. And although I am *low*, yet my message is from *above*, and he that sent me is great and from above. And oh, that he would grant that this my message might be believed!

What if I should tell you, that God told me last night that he would destroy England and lay it waste? What would you say to this, my beloved? It is my message, my meditation is God's word, and he bid me deliver it to you, and he expects an answer from you. I do my message as God commanded me. What say you to it, England? I must return an answer to my Master that sent me. Yes, this very night I must return an answer. For the Lord has appointed a set time, saying, "And the LORD appointed a set time, saying, Tomorrow the LORD shall do this thing in the land," (Exodus 9:5). Why do you not speak? An answer you must give. Do you think well of it? Will you have England destroyed? Will you put the aged to trouble, and your young men to the sword? Will you have your young women made widows, and your virgins defiled? Will you have your dear and tender little ones tossed upon the pikes and dashed against the stones? Or will you have them brought up in Popery, in idolatry, under a necessity of perishing their souls forever, which is worst of all?

Will you have these temples in which we seem to worship God, will you have them and your houses burnt with fire, and will you see England laid waste without inhabitants? Are you well content that it shall be so? I am an importunate suitor for Christ. Oh, do not send me away sad, but speak comfortably and cheerfully. What are you resolved upon? Are you willing to enjoy God still, and to have him dwell *with* you? It is well. I am glad of it if it is so. But you must not only say so, you must use the means, and you must plead importunately with your God. For although his sword is drawn and in his hand, lifted up and ready to strike, yet suffer him not to destroy, but rather to sheath his sword in the blood of his enemies.

I would be glad to see England flourish still. But if desolation does come, thank yourselves for it. It is your own fault if you are destroyed, and not God's. For he delights not in the death of any. We may justly take up the complaint of the prophet Isaiah, who says, "And there is none that calleth upon thy name, that stirreth up himself to take hold of thee: for thou hast hid thy face from us, and hast consumed us, because of our iniquities," (Isaiah 64:7). But this is our comfort—or

Sermon 10: God's Forsaking a People

rather our misery—that we have quiet prosperity, with ease and commodity, our bellies full, our coffers full, and our backs curiously clothed, not remembering the afflictions of our neighbor nations. But all is well with us, and it will serve our turn. And if we do humble ourselves a little, we think it is well. And therefore we play mock-holiday with God and with his gospel, making it our pack-horse.

Well, look to it, for God is going. And if he goes, then our glory goes also. And then we may say with Phinehas's wife: "And she said, The glory is departed from Israel: for the ark of God is taken," (1 Samuel 4:22). So, the glory is departed from England. For England has seen her best days, and the reward of sin is coming on apace. For God is packing up his gospel, because none will buy his wares. God begins to ship away his Noahs, who prophesied and foretold that destruction was near. And God makes account that New England shall be a refuge for his Noahs and his Lots, a rock and a shelter for his righteous ones to run to. And those that were vexed to see the ungodly lives of the people in this wicked land shall there be safe.

Oh therefore, my brethren, lay hold on God, and let him not go out of your coasts. Look about you, I say, and stop him at the town's end, and let not your God depart, O England. Lay siege about him by humble and hearty closing with him. And although he is going, he is not yet gone. Do not suffer him to go far. Do not suffer him to say, "Farewell," or rather, "Fare ill, England."

Therefore, because I will do this unto you, "prepare to meet thy God, O Israel," (Amos 4:12).

Now God calls upon you, as he did sometime upon Jerusalem: "Be thou instructed, O Jerusalem, lest my soul depart from thee; lest I make thee desolate, a land not inhabited," (Jeremiah 6:8). And so we see what the godly have done before us, and now let it be our copy. Let us, with Mary, clasp close about Christ. They have broken the ice; *let us follow them.* This is our day of atonement. This present day is ours, we have nothing to do with tomorrow. We are at odds with God, and this is the day of our reconciliation, this is the day wherein we are to make our peace with our God, and to end all controversies. Let us therefore labor to prevail with God, and that we may not lose his presence, do as the spouse in the Song of Solomon 3:1: "By night on my bed I sought him whom my soul loveth: I sought him, but I found him not." She sought him, but she could not find him. Yet she did not give over, but she followed him until she found him. So, our God is going. And shall we sit still?

Would you have the gospel kept with lazy wishes? Oh no, no. Arise, arise from your downy beds, and fall down upon your knees, and entreat God to leave his gospel to you and to your posterity. Shall we, by our sins, disinherit our infants and posterity of such a blessing, which is or should be the life of their lives, and so have them brought up in superstition? No, no. Lord, we cannot bear this. Oh, give us neither wealth nor any other blessing but your gospel. This is our plea, Lord.

And when we have found God, then let us bring him home to our houses, and there retain him, so that he may be our God and the God of our posterity, in all our and their afflictions. And this will make you rejoice exceedingly. Oh my beloved, carry God home with you, and let him be a Father to you and to your posterity.

[Question] But how may we keep the Lord? It would be worth our labor, for "at thy right hand there are pleasures for evermore," (Psalm 16:11).

[Answer] First, we must be sure to prepare a room for him, for he is a King, and a King you know sends his harbinger before him to prepare a room for him. "Wherefore come out from among them, and be ye separate, saith the Lord, and touch not the unclean thing; and I will receive you. And will be a Father unto you, and ye shall be my sons and daughters, saith the Lord Almighty," (2 Corinthians 6:17–18). So, my beloved brethren, come out of all sinful courses, pleasures, and practices, and you may *expect* God's coming to your houses. And when you sit down by your fires, or lie down in your beds, think this with yourselves: what an equal condition does God propose? It is but only to part with a sin, a lust, a Delilah, which I may very well spare, as well as I may spare water out of my shoes, or a coal out of my bosom. I say, think this with yourself and say in your heart, Will God keep company with me if I will not keep company with sin? Are the terms no harder? This is a good offer. I will at once then bid sin adieu, for now I am upon another bargain. Here is an offer I was not aware of; I will quickly dispatch this bargain and make my peace with my God. And so, if you would have God to be yours, then let your souls and bodies be his by forsaking all sins. And when you shall call, God will come and say, "Then shalt thou call, and the LORD shall answer; thou shalt cry, and he shall say, Here I am," (Isaiah 58:9).

Secondly, as you must prepare a room for God, so you must give him content too. Let God have his will; do not cross him. Where the King is, he will have all things to his mind. Even so it is with God. If he may have his own worship, you please him wondrous well. You must dress his dishes according to his taste. But if you put poison into his meat, if you mingle the traditions of men with God's worship, then you displease him. Lay aside therefore all your superstitions and erroneous opinions of God and his worship, and do it according to his will revealed in his word, and then you please him indeed, when a nation or a soul submits to God and to his truth in all things. "That at the name of Jesus every knee should bow, of things in heaven, and things in earth, and things under the earth," (Philippians 2:10). To bow at the word "Jesus" is not meant; for so to give him the bow is to commit idolatry. But the meaning is, we should worship him in spirit and in truth, humbly subjecting ourselves unto Christ.

Thirdly, as we must give him his mind, so we must give him welcome. If you displease God and look loweringly or sourly upon him, and grudge at God or at his truth, no wonder then if God goes away. And surely this is the sin of England. We bear an ill will to God and his word. And God has done well for this land, and what more could he have done for this land, as he says of his vineyard? "What could have been done more to my vineyard, that I have not done in it? wherefore, when I looked that it should bring forth grapes, brought it forth wild grapes? And now go to; I will tell you what I will do to my vineyard: I will take away the hedge thereof, and it shall be eaten up; and break down the wall thereof, and it shall be trodden down," (Isaiah 5:4–5).

And for all that may be gathered, so it is likely to be with us, if his mercy prevent it not. For are we better than the old world? The same sins that were found in the old world are found in us. Sodom's and Gomorrah's sins were but straws in respect of ours, and yet God rained down fire and brimstone upon them. Tell me, are there not as great sins among us as were in Jerusalem, who were carried captives, their city destroyed, and they a vagabond people until this day? Are we better than other brethren and neighbor nations, that have drunk so deeply of God's wrath? I tell you truly, we are a burden to God. He cannot long bear us, and he will think his burden well over when he has destroyed us. You know all men are glad when their pain is over. Even so it is with God. We are a pain and a trouble unto him. And why should God go continually pained with us, who are worthy to be destroyed?

Then shall England seek peace, but shall not find it. God shall not pity us. Oh, my beloved brethren, what a pitiful thing it is when a merciful God shall show himself unmerciful, when his patience shall be turned into impatience. There is a hard time ere long befalling England, if God in mercy prevent it not. But we do not consider it. Lamentable is our time. Christ wept over Jerusalem: "Saying, If thou hadst known, even thou, at least in this thy day, the things which belong unto thy peace! but now they are hid from thine eyes," (Luke 19:42). Beloved, what do you think we shall do, when *God's mercies are turned into justice?* Look to it, England. The Lord has wept over you in mercy many years. What shall we do when we have leisure to consider, what once we did enjoy? For God's patience is never truly prized until we want it. And then the poor soul will then say: There was a time when we might have been at peace with this patient God, but now he is hid from our eyes. Now the gate is shut, barred, and locked up. Therefore when a people abuse God's mercy, he sends the contrary judgments. And then it will grieve and wound our souls to think, what once we did enjoy. But that soul that will bid God welcome to his heart may go singing to his grave.

Fourthly, you must be importunate with God to tarry, and count it a great favor *if he will stay*. For God has room enough in heaven, and therefore you need not lodge him for want of lodging. But you must be beholden to him to tarry with you (yet in these days men do not love to be beholden). Jacob *wrestled* with God, and by that means he held him until he blessed him. You live under the means, and know the way, and will you not do it? What greater condemnation can there be? And how great will your judgment be unto you, more than unto them that have no means?

And as it was said of Capernaum, so say I to England: "And thou, Capernaum, which art exalted unto heaven, shalt be brought down to hell, for if the mighty works, which have been done in thee, had been done in Sodom, it would have remained until this day," (Matthew 11:23). Thou England, that was lifted up to heaven with means, shalt be brought down to hell. You shall be abused for it. For if the mighty works which have been done in you had been done in India or Turkey, they would have repented by now. And therefore, Capernaum's place is England's place, which is the most scalding, tormenting place of all, if it repents not. And mark what I say: the poor native Turks and infidels shall have a cooler summer parlor in hell than England shall have. For we stand upon high rates; therefore, your torment shall be the more intolerable to bear.

Now the Lord write these things in our hearts by the finger of his Holy Spirit, for his Christ's sake, under whom I would we were all covered. Amen.

FINIS.

Other Works Published by Puritan Publications

Gospel-Fear or the Heart Trembling at the Word of God by Jeremiah Burroughs (1599-1646)

The Five Principles of the Gospel – by C. Matthew McMahon

Gospel Worship, or, The Right Manner of Sanctifying the name of God in General, in Hearing the Word, Receiving the Lord's Supper, and Prayer by Jeremiah Burroughs (1599-1646)

The Necessity, Dignity and Duty of Gospel Ministers – by Thomas Hodges (1600-1672)

Gospel Peace, Or Four Useful Discourses – by Jeremiah Burroughs (1599-1646)

Suffering for the Law and the Gospel – by Thomas Watson (1620-1686)

Walking Worthy of the Gospel – by Nathaniel Vincent (1639-1697)

Other Works

A Gospel-Ordinance Concerning the Singing of Scripture Psalms, Hymns and Spiritual Songs – by Cuthbert Sydenham (1622–1654)

Gospel Music: or the Singing of David's Psalms by Nathaniel Holmes (or Homes) D.D. (1599–1678)

Singing of Psalms a Gospel Ordinance – by John Cotton (1585-1662)

The Law and the Gospel Reconciled – by Henry Burton (1579-1648)

How Faith Works: Rescuing the Gospel from Contemporary Evangelicalism by C. Matthew McMahon

Fit for the Feast – A Guide to the Lord's Supper – by Thomas Tuke (d. 1657)

Christ's Truth Over Heresy – by Richard Allen (b. 1604)

The Way of Holiness – by Oliver Heywood (1630-1702)

Love to God by Thomas Tuke (d. 1657)

Sovereign Grace Against the Gangrene of Arminianism by Richard Resbury (1607-1674)

The Natural Man's Case Stated – by Christopher Love (1618-1651)

Underneath the Blood – by C. Matthew McMahon

www.ingramcontent.com/pod-product-compliance
Lightning Source LLC
Chambersburg PA
CBHW030107170426
43198CB00009B/524